THE PEOPLE OF YOYO

Who we are and where to find us

By Jeremy "Mr. Yoyothrower" McKay

Cover designed by Aimee Coveney
Chapter Art by Christopher Francz
Yoyo Diagrams by Cameron Blair

J.D. McKay
Visit my website at www.jdmckay.com

First Printing: Sept. 2020

For information about bulk purchases, sales, promotions, fundraising, and education needs, please contact J.D. McKay at jdmckayauthor@gmail.com

ISBN-978-1-9991887-8-8

To all the people in my life who inspire me to create.
To every one of the yoyoers I've met or have yet to meet.
You are amazing people, keep being you.

TABLE OF CONTENTS

INTRODUCTION

HI! I'M NEW
CAN I GIVE IT A TRY?
WHAT A STRANGE HOBBY...
WHERE DO I APPLY?
HOW ABOUT A COLLECTION?
VIDEOS ONLINE?
WHAT A WONDERFUL LIFE YOU LEAD!
CAN I MAKE IT MINE?

A yoyo is a magical device. It is a skill toy, a hobby, a passion, and a sport. It can be an object of frustration, determination, and peaceful meditation. Hand-carved wooden disks or titanium carved by a computer-controlled lathe; a yoyo can be both a competitive sport as well as a casual hobby that fits in your pocket. A yoyo is a tool to keep a solitary mind calm or a talisman around which community forms. Folks from disparate backgrounds come together and bring the best of themselves to their shared love of yoyo.

I picked up my first yoyo when I was five years old and have spent my life perfecting the art of... Actually, no. I didn't pick up my first yoyo until age 29, when a yoyo-slinging inspirational speaker entranced my Grade 2/3 class. The students all bought yoyos and I grabbed one so I could learn enough to help get the kids started. At least, that was the plan. Ten years later I have a room in my house dedicated to yoyos and find myself writing books about them. Through yoyo I've made friends, learned skills, and travelled to places I never would have seen.

People have been playing with yoyos for over two thousand years. You have likely played with one or know someone who has. Rock the Baby, Walk the Dog, Man on the Trapeze—these tricks have become part of the English language in a fundamental way. Modern yoyos don't look like yoyos from 30 years ago, but when someone sees me playing they say "Hey, it's the yoyo man!" and ask for a trick by name.

So, who yoyos?

The answer is... anyone who wants to. There's a place for everyone. Yoyo is easy enough to keep one on your desk to bounce up and down for a minute or two during a break, or hard enough to challenge the most intense competitive spirit.

Dazzling Dave Schulte embodies the diversity of interest in this hobby. He's a well-known performer, teacher, and demonstrator. He's spent his career sharing the love of yoyo.

> *I started as a hobbyist in the early 1990s, and then a competitor in the late 1990s. Throughout I was a collector, and to this day I have about 2000 yoyos. I feel now my biggest contribution to the sport is as a teacher. Before I became a full-time yoyo pro in 1998, I was a Tech Ed teacher for middle school. Teaching is in my blood. Now I just concentrate on the yoyo end of things. I excel at helping absolute beginners to master the basics.*

What Dave does is probably the most important job in yoyo—sharing the passion with the next generation.

So, what is a yoyo? A maddening yet addictive childhood toy? That thing your sibling did ALL THE TIME until they broke dad's favourite lamp? Something a person at the office was always playing with? At its core, it's a simple pair of discs on a string that goes up and down. I used to think that's all there was to it, then I dove down the rabbit hole of modern yoyo. This age-old toy has grown in sync with our technological world, but has kept its roots while growing up into something new.

You can walk into a dollar store and find an old-fashioned yoyo. (I don't recommend it. The quality is poor.) Doing a little research and spending a little more will get you a much better experience. If you explore online, you'll quickly lose yourself in a world of "ball bearings" and "Aircraft grade aluminum." Terms like "unresponsive" and "bind" may confuse you. Luckily, you'll also find an online community more than happy to help you choose the right yoyo to get started and videos to teach you everything you need to know.

This book is a guide - an introduction to the modern world of yoyo. Yoyoers from diverse backgrounds share their stories, their joy, and their struggles. I've organized these stories by "type" of yoyoer to provide a framework, but no one fits in just one box. You'll read stories from world champions to average yoyoers taking a break at work to calm the mind with a couple tricks.

A worldwide community has grown around this simple machine. Contest champions shine the brightest, but they are the smallest slice of the pie. Trick innovators, collectors, teachers, leaders, hobbyists, performers... the list goes on. The yoyo world is big enough for everyone. Whether you're four or one-hundred-and-four years old, it's never too late to start.

So many people started their yoyo journey with a school visit from a travelling yoyo performer. That's how I started, so we'll begin with that tale.

How I Started

Unlike many yoyo lovers I began late, at age 29. I may have tried yoyo as a kid, but don't have any memory of doing so. Instead I caught the yoyo bug the same way so many others have—the travelling yoyo-man. I am an elementary school teacher in British Columbia, Canada, and I discovered yoyo when "The NED Show" came to my school. The show involves inspirational storytelling with yoyo tricks as the prop. NED is a cartoon character, but his name stands for "Never give up, Encourage Others, and Do your best." A great philosophy for kids finding their way into a new hobby.

It began on an average day in 2009. One of the perks of teaching is the strange and wonderful performances we get to watch—shows featuring everything from taiko drums to acapella singers to capoeira performers.

One day, a travelling yoyo storyteller performed during a school assembly. They used simple, old-school yoyo tricks to tell an inspirational story. This blew the children's minds, especially when they learned they could buy their very own yoyos. And they did—in droves.

The kids bought out their inventory (they spent over $1200 on yoyos)! Suddenly my entire class was flinging around (and breaking) yoyos. I knew I was going to end up with a lot of upset and confused students with broken yoyos if I didn't do some learning. I decided I had to buy one too, if only to help troubleshoot the children's problems. So, I bought one... then another... and another. It was the classic *"I'll just have one potato chip"* scenario. I picked up a yoyo and 10 years later I still have a hard time putting it down.

Serendipity

Sometimes, you just have to run with whatever life throws at you. When the NED show came through my school, I was the only male teacher on staff. A group of grade 4-5 students wanted to come learn yoyo with me because they "needed a male role model"—at least that's what their teachers told me. I think it was just the mystical lure of the yoyo. Other schools were hit by a temporary craze after a yoyo show, but once the novelty wore off, everyone went back to trading Pokémon cards. My school was different. Yoyo stuck. The kids that stuck with it were REALLY into it. It was all they talked about. They even put together a presentation on the history of yoyo with a slideshow we toured to a few other schools.

A local news station came in and recorded a seven-minute segment on the club that aired on TV. It was always yoyo time. Most days, I could barely eat lunch!

The Kids: My Inspiration

The best part about all this yoyo madness was watching these youngsters grow and develop. They were a diverse group. Some enjoyed collecting and trading, while others created new tricks or trained for competition. They all had a unique take on how to enjoy the hobby. My little group was amazing, and I am in awe of the magic they created.

Extra Strings? I'm a Frayed Knot.

The need for replacement string was the catalyst that brought me out into the wider yoyo community. The yoyo show that visited our school sold five-packs of string, but once that sale was over we needed more. Yoyo string quickly gets dirty and frayed, especially when you are learning harder tricks. The weave becomes full of knots, wears out, and breaks. I'd been fruitlessly looking for yoyos and string in stores when I ran into Gary Li. Gary was a young yoyoer who'd discovered yoyo through the internet. He was at the mall waiting for someone and killing time with yoyo practice. When I spoke with him, he pointed me to two essential resources: the Vancouver Yoyo Club and the now defunct website yoyonation.com.

It turns out that there are large communities of yoyoers on the internet, you just need to know where to look. YoyoNation was an online store and forum, a virtual meeting place for yoyoers around the world. It was there that I bought more string for the school kids and connected with the Vancouver Yoyo Club. An early club member, **Wayne Ngan**, remembers:

> *The very first Vancouver meet I've been to (2008) was me and Dennis. I was late and when I got to the Burnaby Library grass area, I saw Dennis yoyoing all by himself. I went up to him and the two of us yoyoed there for a few hours.*

Over the ensuing years, the club grew and shrunk as new members joined and others moved on. I upended the club by bringing along the noisy, excited kids from my school. Many of the club members at the time were quieter introverts, as is often the case with yoyoers. Our arrival added exponentially to the small group that frequented the club and changed the tone of the meets. It also brought us media attention, as the public loves stories about children doing interesting things. It got to the point where we had dozens of members and news crews were interviewing us.

Contest Fever

Dennis Chui, a founder of the Vancouver Yoyo Club, attended the 2010 Canadian National Championships in Calgary. The organizer that year, Chris Mikulin, convinced Dennis to run a contest in Vancouver. Dennis was a ball of stress, but he put together a fantastic event. We had two divisions: one for experienced competitors and an "Under-13" Junior Division. The day was a huge success and gave us a great starting point for future contests. In subsequent years the contest became an annual event that I often ran as well.

The Holder of the Credit Card

In 2009, yoyos were hard to find in Canada. The internet was the only place you could get anything worth throwing. Becoming a "Yoyopreneur" (yes, that's a word... at least, it is now) snuck up on me. When I found the hobby, the quality of Chinese-made yoyos was catching up to that of USA-made yoyos. They were also available for a fraction of the cost. As the only adult in the group with a credit card, I ended up collecting money and ordering yoyos. When it came time to plan the second Western Canadian Regionals in 2011, I decided to set up a "general store" type table. I brought in a bunch of different yoyos and accessories, and even hand-painted cases.

I continued this trend at the 2011 Canadian National Championship, where I had a table selling gear beside Ray Smith. Ray was just getting his brand, MonkeyfingeR Design, off the ground. We chatted, and he ended up inviting me to join his team as a sponsored player. In that role, I promoted his brand by doing what I knew how to do best: teaching! I began with simple basics and now have YouTube videos teaching over 400 tricks, most of which I've invented. What I love is that every one of these videos has touched someone's life—they've watched it and learned from it, and it's become part of their yoyo experience.

A Business?

Eventually, the point came where I had enough of a presence in the yoyo community that a big opportunity was offered. A Chinese yoyo company called King Yo Star was trying to break into the world market, and they offered me a position as the North American manager of the brand. I thought it would be a fun extension of the hobby. Instead, it ended up being a crash course in running a business— one that has led to unexpected travel and new experiences.

In 2014, my wife and I travelled to Prague for the World Yoyo Championships... and our honeymoon. (Ok, we went to Italy for three weeks for the honeymoon and THEN went to the championships, but I like to brag about my wife, who is so supportive of my yoyo madness. Her joy at seeing me so excited as I explore this passion keeps me moving forward.)

Worldwide Community

Attending this contest was an eye-opening experience. I couldn't believe the extreme level of competition. The international yoyo community is both diverse and tight-knit. During the event, someone from Austria approached me and asked to take a picture with me. It turns out he had learned how to yoyo from my instructional videos on YouTube and was excited to meet me. I felt like an international celebrity!

2014 was the first time in modern history that the World Championships were held outside of North America. The newly formed International Yoyo Federation (IYYF) oversaw the contest. Prague has one of the most active yoyo communities in the world, and it thrilled them to be hosting the event. Players that compete at the world level work as hard as any other top-level athlete. The champions practice four to eight hours per day, honing their skills to a level akin to magic. I learned a lot about the yoyo industry at that event and came home inspired.

Since coming back from Prague, I've built my own brand - Rain City Skills - out of a desire to create yoyos that tell a story. For me, the business is a meeting point between creativity and work. Making connections with people and building a community drive me, and I love it!

The kids who began this journey with me have all graduated high school or are close to doing so. They likely haven't picked up a yoyo in years. I run clubs every year at a couple of schools, bringing in new throwers who join the Vancouver yoyo scene, and continue to become increasingly immersed in the yoyo world.

To this day, everything I do with yoyos is driven by a desire to share, educate, and bring people together.

Individuals all over the world learn yoyo tricks on my YouTube channel. I founded the Canadian Yoyo Association, won the Canadian Yoyo Championship twice, organized over a dozen contests, run businesses, and have done my best to help this hobby grow. Yoyo has been a meditation tool to help me through serious life challenges, and a crutch to get over social anxiety and make connections. My wife takes great pleasure in dragging me towards others, saying, "Look at the cool thing my husband does!" It's how I've found my community, my people, and a place in the world.

For the sake of making this book work, I will generalize various "types" of yoyoers with umbrella terms. Most yoyoers fit many of these categories. Some are driven to collect yoyos, others spend their time developing tricks and innovating. Many yoyo alone as a form of meditation. Still others thrive in large groups, sharing tricks, and being goofy with yoyos. They find passion in teaching and learning from each other. More than anything, yoyoers are average, everyday people. They want to fit in, be accepted, and be happy.

Some journeys are like mine, with people discovering their love of yoyo as adults. Still others played with yoyos as kids and rediscover the hobby later in life. **Michelle Ulep** shares her story, beautifully outlining why I wrote this book:

> I liked the yoyo ever since I was 7 years old when my dad taught me. When I was a kid, you only got one string and if that broke then it's game over. It was a Coca Cola yoyo, and I played with it until it broke. I could make it come back to me and that was a big accomplishment. I stopped when I entered college, but after college I started working and I found a store in our country that sells Duncan yoyos. I bought a Proyo which got me yoyoing again. Tutorials on YouTube were amazing. Yoyo gave me an outlet whenever I'm fed up with life.
>
> I found good friends through yoyoing, and I somehow feel I matter, and I have accomplished something. I hate it when

people tell me that buying an expensive yoyo is illogical and that it's a kid toy. Sometimes I feel they look down on the hobby. My hope is that people will see yoyo as not just a toy, but something you must work hard to be good at. A toy that cheers you up when you buy it or play it or gives you a sense of belonging. That's what I feel when I play with yoyos. I hope there will come a time that people will consider yoyoing a sport since it requires effort and hard work.

Yoyoer, Yoyoist, Yoyo Master, Thrower, Spinner—whatever name we choose, we share something magical. The joy of this hobby is that it's big enough for everyone. This book will take you on a trip through the hearts and minds of yoyoers. Yoyo is a hobby, an art form, a world class sport, a meditation tool, and in many cases a literal life saver. We'll begin with an overview of where to find the modern yoyoer. From there, we'll explore the range of ways to "be" a yoyoer. You'll read stories—some joyous, some heartbreaking—of how the hobby has changed lives for the better. You'll discover how it has been a key to surviving grief, mental illness, and the general trials we all face.

I'm not here to teach you how to yoyo; that's better done through a visual medium like my YouTube channel. Instead, we'll take a journey through a world most don't know exists. This book is meant to remind you that in the internet age, it's still possible to find your place and your people. It's a way to find joy and a sense of accomplishment in a challenging world. Thank you for picking up this book; I hope you'll spot a reflection of your journey somewhere in its pages. If you aren't yet a yoyoer, I hope the tales that follow will stir your curiosity!

Part 1

Where To Find Us

Chapter 1: The Online Community

To me, the best part about yoyoing isn't being able to impress others or nailing a trick, but the amazing community and getting to be a part of it.

– Celine

The modern yoyo world has grown up alongside the internet. Throwers (people who yoyo) watch videos to learn tricks, showcase their skills, and connect with others around the world. Gone are the days when your yoyo community was limited to people you could meet in person. Now, they are people you either found (or more often recruited) by teaching and demonstrating online.

Social media makes it easier to find your community. People stumble upon yoyo through videos on YouTube or Reddit. That's where most of the Vancouver Yoyo Club members come from. Kids spot videos on YouTube or Instagram and then get their parents to buy a yoyo off Amazon. Then they dive into the wealth of tutorials available, from beginner to expert levels. Yoyoers around the world daily. That would have been unthinkable not that long ago.

Yoyo instructor **Patrick Dressel** (aka Hobbygod) bounces around to different platforms for different purposes.

> *I yoyo pretty casually. I am not a competitor and enjoy creating videos for others to watch. A few reviews, but mostly tutorials on my YouTube channel when I have the time (@hobbygod). I spend my time on YoYoExpert forums, Reddit, Instagram, and most recently Facebook for 2a (see appendix A for styles of yoyo). Instagram and Reddit are the best places to get noticed. This helps promote my YouTube channel/tutorials. I talk on the YoYoExpert forums because it feels more personal. A small group of yoyoers on there are very active, and we all seem to talk to each other on a variety of topics. I started learning 2a and joined Facebook to join the 2a group—the main hub where these players talk.*

Social media is a broad term. There are more platforms than can easily be kept track of. There is an ebb and flow of people moving to new platforms as they gain popularity, then moving back as they fade. Community members here talk about why they chose each platform. This is not an exhaustive list, but it gives you a few starting points for your yoyo adventures!

The Yoyo Store Forum

Facebook, Instagram and YouTube may currently be the most likely place to find yoyoers, but it wasn't always that way. Forums hosted by yoyo stores used to be the main hangout. Veteran yoyo pro "**Dazzling Dave" Schulte** reflects:

> *Everything seemed to start with yoyoing.com. The web board was the place to meet other throwers and talk about everything yoyo. There were many others that came along: ExtremeSpin, theyo.com, and yoyonation.com. But I was always on yoyoing.com. That seemed to be the place where most of the experts were. Then it died. I have not replaced it with anything. I guess you could say Facebook has done that, but there are so many players who do not use Facebook. When you post something you never know if anyone really read it unless they engage with you.*

YoYoExpert forum user "**jhb8426**" shares his memories:

Mike Attanasio (otherwise known as YoMike) was the owner of theyostore.com and theyo.com forum (both now defunct). He died in 2010. The store/forum started around 2001 or 2002. Mike was very active on the forum, interacting with members both online and via telephone. There were many active members early on, like the other competing stores/forums. Many close relationships developed on the forum sharing discussions well into the night. Customization and custom paint jobs were popular topics, at least on TheYo.

The main yoyo store forum to hang out on at time of publishing is the Yoyoexpert forum. It was the home of the Vancouver Yoyo Club for many years before we made the move to Facebook.

Forums offer an easy-to-use flexible space to connect, share, and learn from one another. They have sections for sharing yoyo videos, tutorials, and explanations of tricks. The "Buy, Sell, Trade" section allows players to try out a variety of yoyos without paying full retail prices. Of course, there is always the risk of scammers; its' good to get references about people before making a trade. Players regularly ask the community for feedback on themselves and the person they want to trade with. I remember one trade where a neutral third party held the money until the yoyo arrived safely. Store forums are also a good place for younger yoyoers to connect with others, as they are a targeted hobby space. Parents can worry a little less about adult content than they do on Facebook or Instagram.

Bleu Quick shares why they prefer the forum format:

I mainly talk to people on the YoYoExpert forums. Where I'm from, there's no real talk or presence about yoyos. When I stumbled across YYE, it sparked an excitement I haven't had for the hobby since I was in elementary school. I bought my first unresponsive yoyo earlier this year and have been working my way up the trick ladder.

I use the forum to ask questions along the way. Of course there's the Reddit [group] r/throwers. That was never focused enough for me. It all seemed a little impersonal. The people of YYE are very warm and welcoming. People like @Codinghorror (Jeff

*Atwood) have made it a point to make sure I feel right at home.
I tune in daily. Although I may not respond too often, I make
sure I'm plugged in to what's going on in the yoyo community.*

The differences between people are fascinating. Bleu found the
atmosphere on Reddit "impersonal," while many others have the opposite
experience.

Reddit

Reddit is an interesting place. The design is simple and hasn't changed
much since 2005. I've heard it called the "front page of the internet"
because anyone can share content about any topic for all to see.
Facebook and Instagram have complex algorithms dictating what you see
when you log in. Visibility on Reddit is based on user voting. When you
post a picture, a video, or some writing, everyone else gets to "upvote" or
"downvote" your content. If your post gets a lot of upvotes, it stays visible
in the first couple of pages. If not, it quickly disappears.

Reddit consists of "sub-Reddit" groups focusing on single areas of
interest—anything from spearfishing to football to...well...yoyos! For
yoyoers, this sub-Reddit group is called r/throwers. There, diverse yoyoers
from beginner to pro share their tricks and discuss yoyos. When the group
was asked why they chose Reddit, they gave a wide range of answers:

"I can search posts in chronological order"

"I can save posts to look at later"

"I'm already on Reddit every day"

"I like the community here"

"I don't want a Facebook account."

"Brand owners are often on and very approachable."

"I feel my voice is heard."

Celine's story represents the consistent generosity I see in the yoyo
world. Her introduction into the Reddit yoyo community was a warm one.
She reflects:

I bought my first yoyo (a "Recess" First Base) after finding a clip from an online pen spinning forum. I immediately loved it. I found the sub-Reddit for throwers and found others with the same hobby at different skill levels. Beginners all the way to national and world caliber yoyoers can participate.

After a month or so of learning new tricks with my First Base, I wanted to try another yoyo—specifically a metal one. I hopped onto the sub-Reddit and asked for recommendations. People posted helpful replies, but one thrower reached out to me specifically. They were willing to send a Magicyoyo N11 to me, free of charge. I was absolutely floored by their kindness.

When the package came, I opened it to find not just the N11, but three other metal yoyos, a bearing removal tool, several extra bearings, and string. Since then I've seen again and again how friendly and helpful other throwers can be.

The following summer I was in China. I stumbled across a cheap and gimmicky plastic yoyo with hubstacks at a dollar store. I bought it (because why not?) and started playing with it while walking around.

A little girl approached me and wanted to know where I bought it. At that moment I remembered how excited I was to receive my first metal yoyo from a stranger I had never met before. I told her to take it as a gift and seeing the surprised smile on her face made my day. To me, the best part about yoyoing isn't being able to impress others or nailing a trick. It's the amazing community and getting to be a part of it.

You'll find the common theme throughout this book is positivity and inclusiveness. The yoyo community has all sorts, and it isn't all rainbows and sunshine, but we love yoyo and want to spread the joy.

Facebook

When the Vancouver Yoyo Club made the move from the YoYoExpert forum to Facebook I followed along. It's easy enough for people to find the club page. Telling a curious kid or parent to "find the Vancouver Yoyo Club on Facebook" is a lot less complicated than telling them to "make an account on the yoyoexpert.com forum, then find the Vancouver Yoyo Club thread under the clubs and contests thread." It's a good place to find out when meets are happening.

There are more groups than I can keep track of. Trick style specific groups (Offstring Yoyo Nuts, 2a Yoyo), crossover hobby groups (Drink Beer & Yoyo), and even support groups (Throw Therapy). Most yoyo brands have business pages or official fan groups. I have a group called "Mryoyothrower's Minions" to connect with people who follow me.

A popular group is "Yoyo BST & Talk." As the name suggests, it's a place to buy, sell, trade, and talk about yoyos. The challenge with any online community is managing members. A Facebook group is only as good as its moderators (we'll talk more about this later in the community leader chapter).

Instagram

Instagram has grown in popularity in recent years. Yoyo is a visual hobby, so a platform aimed at pictures and video is perfect.

Content on Instagram is organized by "hashtag." Here are a few that were useful at time of printing

#yoyoer
#trickcircle
#todaysthrow
#yoyotricks

It'll take a bit of poking around to find what you need. Contests, brands, and events all set up their own hashtags. For instance, the 2019 World Yoyo Contest used "#WYYC19." You'll fine me with #raincityskills and #mryoyothrower.

When you post content on the site, just add your chosen hashtag to the written part of your post and anyone searching for it will find you!

I've had a hard time seeing Instagram as a place to build community, but I suspect my age is showing there. Many yoyoers say Instagram is their main source of yoyo connections. As Facebook moves increasingly towards paid visibility more people are moving to Instagram. You can still find what you are looking for, and brands or high-profile yoyoers can still be reasonably sure the content they create will be seen. It is definitely worth checking out as a source of inspirational trick videos.

YouTube

YouTube is the easiest place to send new yoyoers interested in learning tricks. There, they will find contest videos, trick tutorials, unboxings, and reviews aplenty.

Parents of younger yoyoers should supervise their YouTube watching. Anyone can put anything they want on YouTube (with some limits), but there aren't any real age restrictions on the content. Unmoderated comments sections of videos can also be unwholesome. Still, as a learning tool, it can't be beat. My advice is to take advantage of YouTube's parental controls and limit what your child can search for online.

With all this talk about the yoyo community online, the one thing I haven't mentioned yet is real-world meeting places. Yoyo is a hobby that tends to attract introverts, but we do enjoy coming together for an event. Even if all we do is stand quietly yoyoing at each other, we share a bond without words. Yoyo clubs and contests bring us together and remind us that we are more than simply names on a screen—we're a real community!

Chapter 2: The Yoyo Club

Yoyo clubs are a lot of fun, but they can be challenging to track down. These clubs are loose knit groups that meet to talk, teach, connect, and revel in the joy of common interest. If you find a yoyo club near you, it'll feel like you've stumbled into a secret society. As with any hobby there is lingo to learn. You'll find us teaching tricks saying things like: "Start with a double or nothing, then pop up over your non-throw hand into a 'Green Triangle,' then out the back and into a whip bind."

I could write an entire book of terminology. Like any sport, the way to learn the language is to play the game.

What happens at a yoyo club? Well, every group is different. If you walk into a Vancouver Yoyo Club meet, you'll find us hanging out in a corner of a small suburban shopping center. The management lets us use the space as long as we are respectful and sign waivers once a year. You'll often see a pile of coats (it's rainy and cold a lot of the year) with a variety of yoyo cases piled on top. People will stand around playing with yoyos, sharing tricks, and talking. You may even find a pair of yoyoers haggling over a trade or sale.

It's rare to find modern yoyos in physical stores. At most, you will find some basic beginner yoyos from one of the big brands. For anyone who wants to try new yoyos, one of the best ways is to visit a club. You can trade yoyos online, but there's always some risk, not to mention the cost of shipping. In person, you know what you are getting.

Yoyo clubs in different cities seem to each have their own flavour. The one thing they all have in common is a willingness to welcome new yoyoers. I think you'll find that when a kid walks up and stares wide-eyed, most yoyo club people will jump to welcome and teach them.

The best part for me is the teaching. I like to show up at club and share my latest tricks, then teach other players the "elements" or parts of a trick. It's exciting to watch as they finally "land" a new trick.

A few club leaders share their experiences:

Wayne Ngan

I've been friends with Wayne for many years now. We once drove 16 hours in two days to visit the One Drop yoyo shop in Eugene, Oregon. He and I take turns running the Canadian Yoyo Championships—one year in Vancouver, the next in Toronto. I asked him to share his experience as one of the leaders of the Toronto Yoyo Club.

I started hanging out with the Toronto Yoyo Club back in 2009 when I moved to Toronto. The club was already pretty well established. I found them through the YoYoNation forums, so I already knew the people there before I moved there. By an awesome coincidence, their yoyo meets happened a five-minute walk away from my house and work. On a weekend afternoon (and I was usually free on weekends) yoyo club for me was just stepping out of my door with yoyo in hand.

What I've noticed over the years was that most people in the club don't stick around forever. They hang out regularly, maybe for a year or a few, and then at some point they don't show up anymore. It's understandable because going to yoyo club meets is an actual commitment. You don't HAVE TO go to yoyo club (I hope not!). You CHOOSE to go to yoyo club. It's like any relationship with people. You need to commit to making it happen.

As people grow older, especially with young adult yoyoers, life priorities change, and sometimes yoyo club moves down the list a bit. Over 10 years—from 2009 when I first joined to present day 2019—the group who make up the yoyo club are almost entirely different! Old regulars fade away, new faces appear. The yoyo club stayed in this 'equilibrium' for 10 years.

We never seemed to run out of new people. I guess this is an advantage of being Toronto with a few million people living in it. Once you set up some kind of social media presence, people just find it. If you live in a major metropolitan area, chances are there are plenty of yoyoers around you. You need only go find them!

Jim-E Pendall

Jim-e Pendall didn't have a nearby club, so he started one! He emphasized that he wanted a club open to everyone, kids and adults alike.

Our club was born out of necessity to find others who also yoyo. Once I saw my daughter begin to take interest in yoyo, I noticed her friends were also intrigued by it. I wanted our club to be as a haven not only to yoyo [and] learn to yoyo, but [also] just to come and feel involved as a community.

Usually I'll arrange meet ups at the library or Big Spring Park. I always have extra yoyos with me and encourage people of all ages to come play. I'm finding people are fascinated. Yoyo brings up memories of their youth. People always stop and take interest—they share stories of how they had this kind or that kind of yoyo as a kid. I'm always hoping to further grow our club here and offer any resources I can. We welcome anyone local, parents, kids, friends of my daughter. Yoyo is creative and fun, and we are always hoping for more people to come by.

Ditch Down 44

The Ditch Down 44 (DD44) club differs from most clubs. They are adult-focused and straddle the line between online and in-person communities. You can only join if you have a tattoo below a "ditch" (i.e., between the elbow and fingers, or below the knee). You must be referred by a current member you have met in person. This means you can't just hang out at home yoyoing; you need to attend clubs or contests! DD44 has a group on Facebook, but seems to be more about connecting in person at contests.

Founding member **Jerret Ulmer** shares the origins of the club.

The idea for a tattoo themed yoyo club came up in a studio in Bremerton, WA called Tattoo Technique. This is where I met John Huber and began my personal yoyo journey, circa 2001. Fast forward seven years. I've moved to St Louis, Missouri. There is a cool contest in Indianapolis at the end of May (MEC 08) set to be a battle format. John flew to St. Louis from Seattle. Along with Adam Lawson, we drove from St Louis to Indy. We had a great time. John took second and we met up afterwards, at a bar for the birthday of another tattooed player we met at the contest.

At the Alley Cat in Indianapolis, we talked about forming a club to bring all yoyoing tattooed adults together. The contest ended, and after a great Korean lunch, the club started with five original members: Adam Lawson, John Huber, Scott Bender, Kyle Pearson, and I. Since that time, we have brought in over a hundred members in 11 countries.

We find people organically, meaning face to face at contests. The meaning of DD44 is simple. Two D's for the letters that start Ditch Down, and D is the fourth letter in the English alphabet so DD=44. The club gives us yoyoing adults a place to play and talk while still being adults. It's turned into a brotherhood, where members turn to each other and help in many aspects of their lives.

Due to a childhood piano lesson related injury, I can't wear rings on my left hand. So, when I got married I got a tattoo for my wedding ring! That was enough to qualify me. I've been friends with members for years (some of them were on team MonkeyfingeR at the same time as I) and I was in. It's a lovely and supportive little community.

Ross Levine

In the 1990s, it was more common to find yoyos in stores, with yoyo pros running classes. Big brands would regularly partner with local stores to host their touring yoyo pros. The times have changed, and with the increase in price of yoyos, stores are less likely to take the risk on stocking them. Ross Levine shares a tale from his youth:

> *I grew up in Redondo beach where there was a kite shop that sold yoyos and held classes. A friend of mine named Julian and I would go and hang out there every Saturday for hours. The teacher and shop attendant was named Yoshi. He worked there most of the afternoon, so if we stayed past the end of the official class time, we'd get a bunch of free learning time. It was a tiny shop with hardly any customers. I imagine Yoshi tolerated us staying so long since we were, at worst, company that he could yoyo with.*
>
> *We went to those classes every Saturday for years and in that time, we watched regulars come and go. People learned to start yoyoing and grew to love yoyoing. Some of the more notable regulars that I saw were Grant Johnson, Alex Hattori, Anthony Rojas, and Alex Kim (owner of Recreational Revolution). I'm pretty sure Yoshi taught or at least heavily influenced players such as Alex Hattori, Grant Johnson, and Patrick Borgerding. Yoshi also did a ton of work with YoYoJam. He judged countless contests in Southern California and elsewhere. Plus Yoshi is an incredible yoyoer himself. I recommend you do yourself a favor and look up some of his 2a Nationals' freestyles.*
>
> *The kite shop isn't selling yoyos anymore, but Yoshi still teaches and inspires generations of yoyoers. His most recent notable student, Justin Dauer, just got sponsored by Duncan. Yoshi is, in my mind, what every yoyoer should be. He's someone that teaches anyone who wants to learn and gives to the community with no expectations.*

Finally, we come to contests—the biggest meetups for yoyoers around the world.

Chapter 3: The Yoyo Contest Community

It was nonstop throwing every day. At any given time, someone would be awake that youcould hang with.

—Mark Montgomery on the World Yoyo Contest

The contest community is a relatively new aspect of the yoyo world. Before the 1990s, contests were pop-up events run by individual brands to promote their yoyos. Contests have grown to become part of yoyo culture.

Many people attend just to see friends, connect with and learn from the pros, and peruse vendor tables. A personal favorite is the Pacific Northwest Regional. I go every year, largely to see friends and learn new tricks.

Serious yoyoers test their skills at yoyo contests. The beginners, the casual players, the introverts—we all find a place in the contest community. Contests are a place to hang out and yoyo together. A breakdown of how competition works is the subject for another book. Here, we'll examine the convention side of these events—the yoyo meeting place.

Pacific Northwest Regional Championships are held at the Seattle Center Armory, which happens to house a food court. My first year attending (and first contest) was 2011. The MC did a mini poll of the crowd, instructing, "Raise your hand if you didn't expect to be at a yoyo contest today." Every year, half of the audience raises their hands. People visiting Seattle Center's museums and exhibits stop in for lunch. Folks see the action on stage and sit for a minute or two -and end up staying for the afternoon.

It would be great if more contests were like this, but most happen in halls or theatres away from the public. It goes to show that yoyo can enthrall a crowd – the crowd just needs to find us first.

Your average yoyo contest includes multiple divisions. Most have a beginner event, either a "Sport Ladder" or "Junior Freestyle." A sport ladder is a list of set tricks one must perform in order. The person who completes the most tricks without errors wins. A Junior Freestyle is more complex. Yoyoers have one minute to showcase their best tricks to music. The championship divisions are similar, often with a longer routine and more emphasis on performance.

No matter how extreme the skill level gets, yoyos will always be toys. I like to include fun, frivolous, and silly games to contests to lighten the mood and give the people offstage a way to be involved. In between the main competitions there are mini games—Walk the Dog race, Rock the Baby battle, or a good old-fashioned Long Sleeper contest. These kinds of events are wonderfully inclusive. Most of the audience know the tricks by name, and beginners can learn them that day. The end result is people of all ages having a blast together.

The Mountain Dew Cup is the single most entertaining thing to happen at a yoyo contest in years (in my opinion). In 2017, the International Yoyo Federation (IYYF) hosted that year's World Contest in Reykjavik, Iceland. Mountain Dew supported the event as a major sponsor. To provide value to Mountain Dew, the organizers added a new event. Each day, 30 minutes before the final event, a special event happened. It was a chance for players to have fun and be ridiculous.

Everyone who signed up received a basic plastic yoyo with the Mountain Dew logo on the side. They had 30 seconds to put on a show, accompanied by a cheesy pop song composed for the event. Modern high-performance yoyos enable players to do amazing things. When faced with a simpler design, the playing field flattens out. It forces people to improvise and be creative. The simplicity of the yoyo led to an emphasis on fun and creativity. Some attempted to do very hard tricks, usually ending in delightful disaster.

The day of the contest finals included a final for the Mountain Dew Cup. The person who won didn't do so with a mind blowing speed combo. Instead, they walked around stage and did a few exaggerated poses. A single sleeper trick followed while they downed an entire bottle of the yellowish liquid, the yoyo spinning all the while. They won the coveted Mountain Dew Cup...a plastic cup of Mountain Dew!

Contests are, at their core, places where the best yoyoers face off. Yet contests are also meeting places for the rest of the community.

The Vendors and Swap Meet

Most yoyoers I've met enjoy looking at yoyos and contemplating their next purchase. Most contest organizers create a space where sponsors can run a table demonstrating or selling their wares.

I've been to contests in Canada where vendor tables weren't an option because of venue rules. It always feels as if something is missing when the vendors section is absent. In 2014, Canadian Nationals was held at West Edmonton Mall. Because it was a shopping center, vendors weren't allowed. Sponsors could have a demo table, but no sales. MonkeyfingeR Design (MFD) was still sponsoring me at this point. They had sent me with yoyos to sell. During the first half of the day, I talked to people and told anyone that was interested, "Psst, meet me in the parking lot...you bring the cash, I'll bring the yoyos." It was really funny doing shady yoyo deals between cars in the parkade.

The shopping element at a competition is part of the experience. People love to try new yoyos, meet brand owners, and score rare deals. Yoyos bring joy, and the creators are part of the experience. Because it is rare to find a good quality yoyo in a physical store, the tables are often the only time you get to try before you buy. Vendors allow clients the chance to ask questions and talk shop. It is also an excellent way for new boutique sellers to connect with current and future clientele.

Another fun memory from that first PNWR was the afterschool program known as "Yoyo University." I remember asking someone, "Who are the kids running around in yellow t-shirts?" The reply made me laugh:

"The Golden Piranhas." Apparently, this group of young enthusiasts would descend on contests and buy out the vendor tables. And they did! They spent half the day getting their yoyos signed by anyone who looked like they were somebody.

The kids mistook me for a pro and asked me for an autograph. At first, I declined, and explained that I was as new if not newer than any of them. But the kids insisted, and so we compromised. I signed their yoyos, and they signed mine. It is one of the treasures of my collection. To this day, I set aside a yoyo and collect signatures from each contest I visit.

The swap meet is another aspect of competitions. Shipping is expensive, so trading yoyos online comes with a cost. People come to contests intending to trade to get their hands on new gear. It's an inexpensive way to test out different styles of yoyo. It's also the core of the hobby for many. People enjoy seeing what kind of deal they can score. Some serious collectors use this time to either showcase their collection or try to find rarities.

Both the swap meet in the practice area and the vendor tables are excellent opportunities for beginners and younger throwers to swap out their first yoyos and explore what may work better. One of the joys of any hobby is exploring the variation in equipment!

The Practice Area

My favourite place at any yoyo contest is the practice area. Having the chance to connect with yoyoers at all skill levels is invaluable. Sure, there are groupings of individuals who know one another. Yet top-level competitors are still just kids playing with yoyos. In general these are kind, friendly people you can talk to and learn from. Most are thrilled to respond to the popular question, "Can you teach me a trick?"

Many people who attend contests don't compete. These attendees are there for the vendor tables, swap meet, and practice area. For many people, this is the only chance they will have all year to meet with other yoyoers in person. There is something magical about watching someone in videos or tutorials and then finally meeting them in person. People hang out in the practice area until they see someone do a cool trick, and then ask if they're willing to teach it. The answer is almost always yes. You meet some of the best people that way. So come to a contest, join the practice space, and say hi. Drink in the yoyo magic!

The World Yoyo Contest

The World Yoyo Contest is where players compete in a structured event for the title of World Yoyo Champion. Attendees travel from all over the world to interact with other real live yoyoers for a 72-hour period of frantic, frenetic, sleepless madness. The seating in front of the stage is usually filled with family and friends. The practice area is where the yoyoers spend their time.

Nathan Crissey sums up the marathon that is the world contest:

You get three hours of sleep for four days and wind up feeling rejuvenated.

Steve Kinder elaborates:

Naps under the stage, 3am shenanigans, not knowing whose room you're sleeping in, not knowing who's sleeping in your room, assembling and testing a lot of yoyos, special edition FreeHands, working 18-hour days, the worst pizza. So many good memories. Worlds were some of the best times of my life.

Jake Bullock remembers one of the earlier years of the contest:

It was a weird hotel on the Orlando Strip. All garbage food places, mini golf, and Disney tourist traps. We rarely left the hotel. There was a little bodega which was our only source of food for four days. They had a microwave for your ramen. Randy Shreeves and I bought a bag of Combos and found a screw or some weird chunk of metal in it, so we took it home and mailed photos to the company and they sent a box of manufacturers coupons for free Combos. We tried to use them at the Rosen the next year and they told us they didn't accept manufacturer's coupons.

Mark Montgomery recalls the early years of the contest in Florida:

It was nonstop throwing every day. At any given time, someone would be awake and yoyoing. There was no way to consume and comprehend the quality everyone brought to the table. Videos weren't as abundant back then, so you were REALLY experiencing a dense amount of new material from a ton of world class players. You also had mad time to kick it with ya homies you only got to see like once a year. It's the same as it is now, but it was just different in that era. Communication wasn't as accessible as today. It was good times.

It's hard to explain to modern yoyoers how little video we had access to even 10 years ago. YouTube was new, and few throwers had the equipment, skill, and knowledge required to film decent video.

The contest is also a time for hijinx. I remember seeing a video of people running around, cutting the strings of players in mid-trick during the 2011 World Contest. A prank I'm sure resulted in screams of horror, as a valued yoyo went rolling away into a crowd.

Connor Sewel admits:

Josh Yee, myself, and a few others were getting into shenanigans when one of us cut the other's string while they were doing a trick. It got out of hand and we stalked our friends, avoiding higher end yoyos (sorry Eric Tranton, I feel bad to this day). We'd be like 'Hey, show us a cool trick.' Then in the middle of the trick, they would get their string cut.

Daniel "Zammy" Ickler sums up the power of the community in his memories of the 2018 USA National Contest:

On the real, it's kinda crazy to think I'd ever make it to another yoyo contest. It's increasingly difficult to travel, due to this little thing called 'adulting.' My job keeps me stuck in central Wisconsin, so this entire trip was a pure miracle. This miracle blossomed many great opportunities and experiences thanks to the countless people along the way.

From Wednesday June 27th, until Monday July 2nd, it was a wild ride filled with emotions, going up and down, literally like a yoyo. That's just how it was fated to be. Overall, I will say that this was wanted, this was needed. I NEEDED to be at this contest. It was held at the Midwest regional of the United States for the very first time. To see history live before my eyes made my experience incredibly special, but outside the event was even better. All the get-togethers, hangouts, eating in various spot—all of it.

When I arrived at the contest on Friday, there were tons of people around me, playing Möbius style (one Zammy developed), left and right. It was a powerful moment for me.

Should you attend a big contest and dive into the frenzy of yoyoing, one thing to beware of is 'Post Contest Crash.' Three days of bad food, not enough sleep, and way too much fun will cause burnout. Plan for a few days of sleep, good food and light exercise.

Mason DeVriend concurs:

I couldn't peg it to any specific moments, but post contest depression always hits me tough. My happiest time has to be the night after the contest, a whole evening of nothing but good chilling.

The contest is a nexus of yoyo, a place where people come together. But who are we? Not everyone who yoyos competes. So, what else do we do? The rest of this book answers that question.

Part 2

The People of Yoyo

Chapter 4: Why Do We Yoyo?

When researching for this book I asked people across the internet this very question. The answers weren't all that surprising:

"It helps me relax during a break at work."

"Yoyo helps me improve hand-eye coordination."

"Yoyoing helps calm me when I'm stressed out."

"It's something to fidget with when I'm feeling antsy."

Yoyo can be a great way to take a break from screens, or to gain satisfaction from the challenge of learning complex tricks. It can also be an artistic endeavor involving video, photography, yoyo modification, and performance.

The comment that I liked the most was: "I love being able to see the faces of the kids who see me yoyo." That's a big motivator for me as well. I could write pages of reasons why people yoyo. Everyone has a different need/want/desire that drives them to carry around a yoyo. You'll meet teachers, performers, competitors, leaders, and more. Some are casual yoyoers who just throw from time to time to let off steam. Others practice for hours each day.

Yoyoers start in different places and grow in a variety of ways, but we tend to share a desire to explore the hobby. Not everyone has the drive to compete, but few pick up a yoyo and keep doing the same thing every day. While I've divided the following section by "type" of yoyoer, you'll find that no one fits a single box.

Chapter 5: The Hobbyist

In the interest of starting big and working my way down, I'm starting with the Hobbyist. It's where most of us start. Few of us have the drive to become a World Champion. The Hobbyist might pick up a yoyo a few times a week or carry one around every day. They may have a hundred yoyos or only one. They find yoyo and it fits a hole in their lives they didn't know needed filling. Some learn a few dozen tricks, adding a new one a few times a year. Others learn everything they can and become incredibly skilled.

The interesting thing about yoyoers is that if you ask most if they are good at yoyo, they downplay their skills. A yoyoer who says "I can 'only' do these three dozen tricks" is like a pianist who says "I can only play these three concertos." Relative to the top-level musicians, I'm sure that's not much. However, from my perspective—as someone who never made it past the second Beginner-level piano book—it's downright magical! When you look up at the World Yoyo Champion, you might feel your skills are negligible. I prefer to focus on the reaction of a kid who has never seen modern yoyo before. For them, the simplest tricks look like magic.

Ivan Barnard acknowledges the split between these two attitudes:

I just learned a laceration (yoyo trick), which already puts me leagues ahead of the non-throwing public. By no stretch of the imagination could I be called good.

Peter Hunter has a more optimistic perspective:

I'm better than I was. Am I as good as that guy on stage? Heck no. But I enjoy myself and that's all that matters. For the record I know half as many tricks as I have yoyos, and that's fine with me!

You can be passionate and knowledgeable about a subject without being the best. Peter spends a fair bit of time in the online yoyo world, interacting and making friends. He shares his knowledge and has something to contribute.

One of the fun things about yoyo is the attention it garners. For some people, that's not a good thing. But for people like **Angelo Alfaro** it is a plus:

I am a casual yoyoer, but I want to become more than that, a pro. I think I fit in this category because I yoyo every day and I love it. I started yoyoing earlier this year. My sister and I were cleaning up our room and found an unresponsive yoyo that my mom bought but never used. I took out a knot and threw it. People call me the 'Yoyo Master' at school because of how often I play at school. People started to gain more respect for me. It feels great.

It's amazing how much yoyoing can change a life. Respect is hard to earn as a kid, and if you are lucky, yoyo will do that for you.

I asked the community where and when they yoyo. The answers ranged from "only at home" to "anywhere I can." Some sneak in a few minutes of play before or after work, or on their lunch break. The responsibilities one has to a spouse and/or kids might make yoyoing challenging. For most people, a yoyo seemed to be something to throw in the pocket, on the belt, or in the bag to play with during a spare moment.

Competition is a strange thing. Some thrive in the spotlight, while others shy away from it. Yoyoers were asked why they choose not to step out onto the stage - lack of time or money was a common answer; life and work don't leave space for travel or the ever-increasing cost of competing in contests. Others felt like they will never be ready. For most recreational yoyoers, it's too stressful.

Eli Cooper echoes most yoyoers in the world with this statement:

I yoyo because it is a fun, calming experience. I get satisfaction when I learn a new trick or hit a hard one. Sometimes after a very hard day, I will come home and hit a difficult trick, and it will be so satisfying. I keep yoyoing because it is fun and rewarding, and I don't have a reason to stop!

A yoyoer who goes by the screen name "**Argonaut**" found his passion in yoyoing. Goals are important in life, as humans are at our best when we are striving towards something.

It has made me happy playing yoyo and learning new tricks, so I told my friends how fun yoyo is! I want to share with other people that yoyo is not just a simple toy—there is more to it!

When I feel down at school, I can't wait to get back home to play with my yoyo. Learning new tricks makes me happy for some reason. Yoyo looks hard, but when you play, train, and learn new tricks you will find yourself joyful.

I want to go to a yoyo contest one day and even if I lose, I will keep trying until I get first [place]! After that, I'd like to make an easy-to-use yoyo for beginners. I'd name it 'Argonaut' because it means a hero who never gets down until he wins.

Joseph Aldrich shares his excitement at the friendships he's found and the community that has welcomed him:

I love hobbies but this one I fell in love with. I was new to yoyoing and reached out on Facebook in my neighborhood. I met a guy named Jonathan who was very good. We found two more yoyoers and we live in a small city and decided to meet.

My friend Jonathan had a cool yoyo collection. I only had a few yoyos at the time. He let me try all the different yoyos. One that stood out was called The Ducc. I informed my wife that I wanted that yoyo for my birthday which was months away.

Several weeks later Jonathan sent me a text that his wife had surprised him with a trip to the World Yoyo Contest in Cleveland. I was excited for him and I asked if he would get me an autograph from Dylan Kowalski (a popular yoyo reviewer). He said that he would.

I was at home watching footage from Dylan's YouTube channel. I was super excited; my ADHD was off the chart and I'm starting to realize how amazing it is to be able to go to the contest. So Jonathan and I are texting back and forth, and he says, 'I got you a surprise.' He sends me a pic of him and Dylan and a pic of this pack of Zipline String with a note and Dylan's autograph saying 'Sorry you couldn't make it. Thanks for watching.' I was so excited.

Now comes the best part. Jonathan, this guy I've only met once, and only known for two months, sends me another message. He texts me and says 'I've got you another surprise. Tell your wife not to get that birthday present and I'm not sending you any pics.'

To be honest, I sat there for a while with my jaw dropped. I didn't know what to say. I couldn't think of words good enough to express how grateful I was. Long story short when he got back home, he came by during his lunch hour to give me the gift. It was a beautiful Rain City Skills "Ducc" yoyo (pink splash Darkwing edition) and to top it off it was autographed by Mr. Yoyothrower!

He mentions "The Ducc" a couple of times. It's a yoyo that epitomizes the Hobbyist. It was a yoyo release of mine a couple years ago. A moment of insanity – it was designed by committee. We designed a yoyo through a series of Facebook polls. The yoyo isn't a competition design, it's a fun yoyo to throw in your pocket. The name comes from an inside joke about ducks in the BST&Talk group on Facebook. It's all about the fun.

I've since connected with Joseph through Facebook. He once wrote a song for me, which sounds like a cheesy thing until you hear it. The man has a talent for writing promotional music, to the point where I hired him to write a theme song for one of my sponsored players, Luna Harran. I'm surprised again and again by the random connections I've made with people through yoyo.

The Hobbyist exists at the opposite end of the spectrum from the Competitor—the player who catches the yoyo bug hard and wants to push themselves to the limits. Competitors find themselves drawn to the stage. They step up into the spotlight with a choreographed routine and prepare to wow the judges and audience over and over again. By contrast, the Hobbyist is the easiest type of yoyoer to be. Just relax and enjoy.

Chapter 6: The Collector

Great joy can be found in collecting the tools of a hobby. Yoyoers want to try everything they can get their hands on, and many succumb to the urge to amass the biggest or best collection. For me, collecting was almost a phase I had to work through. A few brands hold sentimental value (General Yo, SPYY, CLYW, MonkeyfingeR), but mint (perfect) condition throws don't appeal to me. I wanted to play with my collection and be comfortable letting others try them.

The few exceptions to this rule are my MonkeyfingeR Design throws. I received a special edition of each release with my name on it while I was on the team. I always bought a second one to play with. I continued to collect until I got to where I was no longer using every yoyo in my collection.

My big revelation came when I started up Return Top Shop. It turned out I wasn't so much interested in collecting yoyos as I was addicted to getting new ones in the mail. A bonus of having the store is sampling everything I stock. I'm now trying to thin out my collection and get rid of anything that isn't personal or hold a memory.

Running my own yoyo brand has left me packing around the yoyos I release so I can take photos—like the one I just took with a yoyo beside my iPad and brownie at the coffee shop where I'm writing this. You can't run an online business without feeding the social media monster! This means the other throws in my collection don't get the belt time they once did.

You'll find that the reasons people collect (and what they collect) vary from person to person. I tracked down some collectors and asked them to share their reasons for collecting.

Tim Chinn

A few years back Tim kindly invited me to stay with him while I was in San Francisco attending a contest. His spare room is also his yoyo collection room. I slept under a giant Ewok about to toss yoyos at me from his hang glider, surrounded by yoyos displayed as art pieces. I asked Tim if he could articulate why he collects. His answer was surprising:

Well, no. And I think you will find that's a common answer.

I asked a better question: What do you get out of having a collection?

I get something interesting to decorate my house with. It started with my photography. There are a series of black and white photos on my wall I took and developed myself using a darkroom. You can go to Target and buy photos to hang, but each of mine tells a story. It was the same with yoyos. I started with the handmade wooden cases in the stairway and it grew from there. You'll notice they aren't even grids; they are displayed in more of an hourglass shape. The ones in my office aren't all level; they are arranged in an uneven curve down one wall and up the other.

His collection is a work of art in and of itself. He has even hand crafted his own display cases. His passion for yoyos merged with his love of Star Wars. On his ceiling, as I mentioned, he has a two-meter-wide Ewok hanging from a glider he crafted himself. It's a scale replica of a toy from when Return of the Jedi came out. The only difference is that the Ewok's bandoliers are full of toys, and instead of dropping rocks, he's dropping yoyos—the YoYoJam "Hitman" to be precise and very appropriate. Unique displays adorn his walls—a pair of arms mounted to the wall doing a Trapeze, a Velociraptor bursting out of the plaster with a pair of *Despicable Me* "Minions" yoyos in its hands. Some collectors keep their collections pristine. When I visited Tim, he insisted I pick up and play with his yoyos. He doesn't collect yoyos for the sake of resale value. His collection revolves around personal stories. Many of his yoyos have been modified, by himself or friends, for aesthetic reasons. These changes devalue the collection, but they are priceless to him.

Matthew Ciurleo

Matthew has a very different perspective on his collection. For him, it's about the history of the sport. He collects modern era throws but loves the hunt for something rare and hard to find. Many of the yoyos he mentions I've never even heard of!

I came into yoyoing in 2007, but only started collecting in 2013, when I discovered yoyos from the late 90s. Mid-2000s throws are my favorite, and I was looking for a painted CLYW 'Peak.' I asked an owner to trade but he only wanted a Crow'd Fusion (which he's found by now). Doing research and learning all about the cold fusion and isotope variants was fascinating. I was never a fan of anything flavor of the month which is pretty much 99% of today's market. So collecting old throws made yoyoing so much more fun.

In a nutshell, I guess the amazing history got me started. I enjoy having and displaying throws, but it's the hunt I love. Most collectors would probably agree. In my eyes there's a distinction between collector and accumulator. The latter cares more about having and lacks focus in the collection. I spent eight months trying to find a USA Hatrick a few years ago, one year for an OG Peak, six months for a mint TiWalker, and several months tracking down the complete Dert line. There was nothing more satisfying than finding those throws and holding them in front of me. The yoyos I'm hunting for now are old Proyos and mid-2000s organics. I was fortunate to find a huge collector leaving the hobby behind. He let a lot of stuff go for pennies on the dollar.

Most of my old Proyos came from him (Gold Fusion/GF GT, all isotopes, nucleus, Crow'd Fusion, LE CF, etc.). They are some of my prized possessions. Like I said before, the history of Proyo and its influence drew me in. I prefer organic throws, so mid-2000s are my second focus. Old General Yo throws and CLYW Peaks are my favorites. The tough to find throws like Kyo's original TiPhiter and Doc Pop's The End are true gems.

It's the stories that get me. That's why Derts are probably my favorite line ever. A guy making throws for a small club in his garage. What's better than that? They are close to impossible to acquire. I've been lucky enough to find a dozen, but only six of the ten different models. I own about 80 yoyos, but quality is more important than quantity to me. Having those requirements has kept the size of my collection in check.

Matthew lists off a lot of different yoyos and brands that I've never heard of. We tend to find something we like and chase after it. Much of the yoyo world operates at the boutique level, which gives collectors plenty of treasures to chase!

Aloysius Grady

Not everyone collects intending to build a fancy collection. Aloysius Grady purchases yoyos as souvenirs of his travels. For him, it is the hunt for something novel that keeps him going.

When I was a little kid, I visited some old battleship or carrier turned into a floating museum. It was a family vacation, and I think it was to one of the Carolinas. I don't remember the trip very well, but I remember the cedar yoyo that I got in the gift shop. I remember the smell of the wood and the smooth feel of the finish in my hand. Why I picked that item as my souvenir I'll never know, I couldn't even yoyo back then. That was the yoyo I learned on! Ironically, I lost it, and it is not part of the collection that followed.

For me it is about the chase. After that cedar naval ship souvenir, I started picking up yoyos at tourist traps. Soon I was searching them out and checking the honky-tonk shops. It became an obsession. Every time I went to a new city or country, my top priority was finding a yoyo to commemorate the trip. When I was a kid, it was easy. Every roadside, boardwalk, and gift shop sold a cheap wooden or plastic yoyo with name of the city, state, or museum stamped on it.

It's lot of work to find them and I don't always succeed. Sometimes I even cheat and buy an old novelty yoyo from a place I have visited. A golf ball display case on my wall displays my favorites, but most are piled into a big decorative bird cage that someone gave me. Last time I counted (a few years ago) it was over 300. I keep saying I will organize and display the collection, but I never get around to it. Finding them is the fun part.

I don't just collect, I use yoyos. Tournament championship isn't in my future, but I can do a couple tricks. I own a nice aluminum and few quality wooden ones that I play with, and some Star Wars, Star Trek, Batman novelties. I've even acquired a few weird designs shaped like footballs and donuts. People give yoyos as gifts. I have a silver-plated yoyo from Tiffany's that was a present. Still, most of my collection is tourist yoyos from places I lived or visited. Plastic Eifel tower yoyo from Paris. Wooden Whisky Heritage Museum yoyo from Dublin. Pinocchio yoyo from Rome. One of my favorites is from Saratoga Springs, NY. I was sent by my old employer to work there for a month, and the people I worked with learned of my collection. They couldn't find one for me and bought just a regular wooden yoyo and wrote Saratoga on it. I love that yoyo.

Let me tell you one more story. I was staying in Nice, France and took the train over to Monte Carlo. I figured I had no chance of finding one there, but at the Christmas Market, a man was selling woodcraft and he had a yoyo. We talked, and I explained my excitement at finding it. When he heard this, he refused to sell it. He said it was not worthy of my collection. He insisted I come back the next day, and he would make me his best yoyo that night. The one he had was good enough, as it was for the collection, and not for use. Still, he did not give me an option. I was done in Monte Carlo but wanted that yoyo, so I complied. Sure enough, the next day he gave me (for free) a perfectly balanced beautiful handmade yoyo. That one has a place of honor in the case.

I want, but will never own, the actual yoyo that the astronauts took up on the space shuttle for their televised experiments. That would hit all the collector buttons. I would also like to get my hands on one that was actually used by Tommy Smothers.

Yoyos make great travel memories! They are small and practical. I don't take it to the extremes that Aloysius does, but I hunt out yoyos where I can. Few things compare to that moment of delight when I find yoyos in a shop. It means local kids are yoyoing, which is a wonderful thing!

Cliff Adams

It's delightful when someone who yoyoed decades ago re-discovers the sport in its current form. It's like discovering a childhood joy all over again. Cliff Adams has seen the changes in technology and never lost his love for the toy! For him, the modern design is what brought out his inner collector.

I grew up in the 1950s when the Duncan experts would visit elementary schools. They would show off tricks at recess and lunch breaks. Occasionally they'd hand out coupons toward buying Duncan yoyos. It took me until 1961, after getting a Duncan Mardi Gras, before I could make a yoyo sleep and return. I got good at looping tricks with that Mardi Gras, but I lost it when my family moved while I served in the Air Force.

Cut to 1999/2000, when McDonalds sold various Yomega yoyos for $1.99. I collected them all, including getting one with the coupon for a free Powerbrain in one. I still have all seven, plus an additional six, still sealed in the boxes. When I was throwing them, friends gave me yoyos, including the re-released Duncan's, for birthdays and Christmas.

I have ignored yoyos since, but in late 2017, I began working on the Sunday school play for my church. That year we performed a version of Horton Hears a Who. We needed a very small student to be Jojo, the yoyo thrower who saves Whoville.

I rediscovered yoyos. Modern unresponsive yoyos and the beauty of metal yoyos, aroused my (heavy) collector's instincts.

(I have collected guitars, basses, ukuleles, comic books, science fiction first editions, and other stuff my entire life.)

I now have 115 yoyos in the collection, including a newly bought Duncan Mardi Gras (not the same color as my 1961). Unresponsive yoyo string tricks are my current challenge. The first bind came easy, but I am slowly learning to land a sideways throw on the string...it will come, I hope soon.

I expect another three yoyos in today's mail, two new ones and one from a BST transaction. Some of my oldest yoyos date back to the 1950s, others were just released. I throw like a beginner used to nothing but looping yoyos. But I can feel a vibe and notice when my throw is crooked, and the yoyo spins at an angle.

One yoyo (of which I bought two) that seems to fit my toss well and correct my incompetence is the MonkeyfingeR PixelApe. Those are the yoyos I compare all new ones in my collection to. I suspect one of those will be the yoyo I get my breakthrough on hitting string tricks regularly. It's the same feeling I had when I was 12 and learning how to play guitar. I know what I need to do, but my muscles aren't caught up to my brain yet. This is amazing fun.

I totally understand the lifetime collector bug Cliff describes. When I was younger, it was G.I. Joe action figures. Later, I moved onto Lego sets. Guitars followed, and now yoyos. Who knows what might come next!

David McEvoy

David is a mix of our previous collectors. He is also an example of the wide age range that exists within the community. He's been playing with skill toys for decades. Modern yoyo captured his attention and ignited his collector bug. He collects for himself, for the joy of having the collection.

I'm the fourth child (second boy) in a family of eight kids. We were 'inner city' but we didn't know that. My dad was a postal worker and often a security guard for additional income. He worked nights because it paid five cents per hour more, and that extra nickel was important.

My mother was an office worker when she wasn't at home with us. I remember a loving, happy childhood. We did chores but didn't get an allowance. At the time we would collect pop bottles for the two-cent deposit. A candy bar cost five cents and twenty cents worth of penny candy was quite a lot.

I don't remember the price of a Duncan yoyo at the time, but it was close to a dollar: a real luxury, (remember, a candy bar was only five cents compared to close to two dollars today). There were also cheap wooden off-brands that were a waste of your quarter.

No one ever came to our school to do a demo, so I don't remember how I got started. I played with tops more than yoyos as they were only 15 cents. We learned the simple tricks from other kids because there was nowhere else to learn them. Eventually I got a genuine Duncan Imperial yoyo. The tricks you could do were limited to things like 'Walk the Dog,' Inside and Outside 'Loop the Loop,' 'Around the World,' and 'Over the Falls.' If you managed a long enough sleeper for 'Rock the Baby' you were really good!

I remember getting bored enough that I put a 10-foot (three meter) string on the yoyo and would do the 'forward toss' trick to knock down Tin Cans.

After age 12, my friends and I moved onto other things and the yoyo went in the junk drawer. I'd occasionally pull it out when I saw a kid with a yoyo, but that was it until much later in life.

I continued to purchase yoyos when I found a good deal. Stores like yoyosam.com, yoyostorerewind.com, and yoyoexpert.com are my main source of new throws. I found a 'Mystery Box' on YoYoSam, marked down from $29.99 to $19.99. It had an

'Anarchist' yoyo and a $5 off coupon in it. I bought a second box that had a 'Rush' yoyo in it which was a steal (Retail Value $75)!

In January 2018, I somehow found the Facebook Buy/Sell/Trade & Talk group. I discovered there were others like me! I ended up learning more about yoyos and brands than most people need to know. A perfect storm of coincidence accompanied this. I'd lucked into a payoff on Penny Stocks (low cost-high-risk investments), which combined with a good Xmas bonus. This left me free to buy every yoyo I could get my hands on. I sometimes think this has gotten out of control as I'm now up to over 200 yoyos, but it's my spending money. I don't have other common vices, so there are worse things to spend money on. Every time I think I should slow down, I find another deal or another yoyo maker releasing something I need to have.

For me, collecting is about getting deals and having the collection. I don't display it or post pictures and to be honest, I don't even remember the name or brand of some of the yoyos I've acquired. But I enjoy them anyway.

About six months after being interviewed, David jumped into the yoyo market himself. He made two yoyos and sold them directly. He told me he wasn't starting a brand; he just wanted to make the one yoyo that was just right for him and share it. One of the wonderful things about the internet right now is that folks can do just that—small batch, single release. More fodder for the collectors to track down a decade from now!

Lucky Meisenheimer

Lucky's career as a physician financed the world's largest yoyo collection. It takes up an entire floor of his home and then some. His journey has turned him into something of a historian, keeping track of artifacts from previous eras. He even wrote a book—*Lucky's Collectors Guide to 20th Century Yoyos.* It's a detailed work, including a history of yoyos and photographs of many of the most collectable pieces. A copy of this book is in the collection at the Smithsonian Institute! I asked him to share a bit about his desire to collect the story of yoyo.

I became fascinated with the history of the yoyo. The era of the Duncan demonstrator ended in the early sixties when I was a kid. I never knew of or experienced the rich history of yoyo contests, which dated back to 1928. My interest was fed by the lack of information on the modern yoyo. Every yoyo has a story behind it. Collecting has allowed me to piece together and preserve some of those stories we would otherwise have lost.

When I started collecting, it was the chase I coveted. The idea of preserving an important piece of Americana later took over as my reason to collect. I enjoy sharing information and hope to inspire others to become collectors as well.

I am indiscriminate—I collect yoyos of all types and eras and the associated yoyo memorabilia, such as string packs, posters, videos, old catalogs, contest awards. The list goes on! My favorite are the yoyos and memorabilia from the 20th century.

Folks often ask, 'Since you have the Guinness Record for the largest yoyo collection, are there any yoyos you don't have? Which is the one you would like to get next?' My answer is there are thousands of yoyos I don't have, and the one I want is the one not in my collection. That is the best thing. You will never have them all! There is always something out there with an interesting story to keep the fire going.

Every year at least one parent at my school asks me, "How many yoyos does my child need?" The answer is that every kid NEEDS to own one yoyo. After that, it's a question of want. There are so many worse things to be spending their money on! Lucky concludes with a sentiment shared by many yoyoers:

You can never have too many yoyos!

Lucky continued writing and released a science fiction novel called *The Immune* which I read and enjoyed. He also wrote a book called *The Zombie Cause Dictionary,* which accompanied a series of short documentary-style films of the same name. Yoyoers often have the most fascinating collection of interests!

Chapter 7: The Teacher

The Teacher is a central figure in the yoyo world. These are often the people who introduce potential yoyoers to the hobby. They guide us through our development and inspire us to learn and improve. YouTube has dramatically altered the way people learn. It is crazy to think that less than 20 years ago it didn't exist. If you wanted to learn to yoyo, you had to meet someone who knew how, or learn from pictures and text in a book or from a mail order VHS or DVD.

It's exciting to create a new trick. The excitement of finding an audience to share it with is inspirational. Getting feedback from friends or yoyo pros by sharing your new trick on YouTube pushes you to grow and excel.

I started making tutorials shortly after joining team MonkeyfingeR Design. Competition wasn't going to be my strong point; I was still too new. I needed something different. So, I put my teaching degree to work. André Boulay's videos on YoYoExpert inspired me. He made learning fun and easy. My early tutorials were simple, shot with a low budget video camera. I tried to break down the tricks and explain them in detail. My focus is providing elements for others to build on rather than teaching long combos.

I put this content out on YouTube and right away started making tens of dollars from ad revenue! Okay, maybe not quite living the dream, but that isn't the point. I made tutorials because it was a way for me to connect with the community and carve out a spot for myself. At present, I don't have ads active on my tutorials (except where YouTube puts them because of music use). There are others who do a better job of explaining, filming, and editing, but I'm happy with what's been achieved.

I think I've taught more original tricks than anyone else. The only person I know who could argue with that is Steve Brown. In 2011, he went batty and committed himself to filming a trick a day for an entire year. Each day, he released a video—first performing the trick, then repeating it in slow motion so the viewer could try to learn it.

I learned what an epic undertaking it was when following in his footsteps in 2015. I created a Canadian version of his project called "Trick a Day, eh?" Instead of doing it all myself, I invited yoyoers from across Canada to submit videos and join in. During this time, my wife and I drove across the eastern half of Canada. We started in Toronto and made our way through Quebec, New Brunswick, and PEI, all the way to Cape Breton. At every stop, we met with any yoyoers I could track down. Most of them were more than willing to have me film them doing tricks.

I spent the trip teaching everyone who was willing to learn. One particular campground presented a missed opportunity due to inclement weather. We'd just spent five nights camping in the rain in Halifax, Nova Scotia. Everything was soaked. We set up at the new campground in Cape Breton and crossed paths with a family the next spot over from us. Their kid spotted me yoyoing and came to check it out as they were heading out for lunch. I said I'd hook him up with a yoyo when they returned. In the interim, my wife and I decided we'd had enough of being cold and wet, and she tracked down a cabin at a nearby hotel. The warm was too enticing, so we packed up and left. In hindsight, I wished I'd left a yoyo with the office to give to the kid.

Some cities had an existing club; in others, I stumbled upon the local yoyo community by accident. Halifax was the best example of this. One of my wife's Facebook friends hired us to perform at a small street festival. As our time ended, a fellow lost his mind with excitement that there was someone else there with a yoyo. He owned one but had broken his last string. I gave him the strings off the yoyos I had on me to keep him going!

These days, my outreach and teaching time is split between my business (tutorials made to promote my yoyos) and my work with schools. I run a club at my school every year and try to support other interested teachers. I run the local Vancouver Yoyo Club that meets once or twice per month and teach anyone who shows up. This is how the sport grows!

Some yoyo teachers are like me, sharing online in their spare time or helping the local club. Others have made a living out of sharing the joy of yoyo! The following pages give you a sampling of the people who teach the world to yoyo.

Dale Oliver

Dale Oliver made a career teaching a school program called "The Science of Spin." His work has influenced many of today's top players. He contributed to the shift to the modern freestyle competition format. Yet his time spent visiting schools is what he is most proud of.

A man once asked me, 'Why in the world would you choose a job like yours? Why do you waste your time in such a silly way?' I told him I brought joy to children and I could not think of a more satisfying way to spend my days. I've taught half-a-dozen World Champions. All of them have said their lives were much richer because of the yoyo. They now have friends from all over the world and have achieved a status far beyond their expectations.

Here is a bit of a summary of what he talked about in schools.

Everything spins, including our world. The physics of spin are all around us, in everything we play with and use. Tops and yoyos are simple gyroscopes. The circular motion gives them their stability. You can find gyroscopes in toys, scientific instruments, and stabilizers in ships and space vehicles. Navigational aids in airplanes and ships. Arrows, bullets, and footballs use spin to make them more accurate. A Frisbee won't fly six feet without spin.

Flywheels are part of thousands of different motors. One of the interesting things about flywheels is the weight distribution. A solid wood top will not revolve as long as a hollow plastic or metal one. It is the weight distribution to the outside rim that makes it more efficient. A Frisbee can be thrown a little over 300 yards, but you can throw an Aerobe (a flying ring) a quarter of a mile (actual record). The only difference is that the Aerobe's weight is around the rim.

These are the physics involved in the yoyo.

- *friction*
- *distribution of mass*
- *gyroscopic stability*
- *rotational inertia*
- *planes of spin*
- *potential and kinetic energy*
- *leverage*

I cannot count the times that teachers and principals thought me a science teacher after watching The Science of Spin.

The physics of yoyos are fascinating. I'm all for anything that gets kids thinking about science, but adding in yoyo is just magical! Oliver's ability to inspire through science is itself inspiring!

Most yoyo lessons are now taught online, but nothing can replace a yoyo master at your school. Local yoyoers in Vancouver start on YouTube and then track down the club. Here are a few people who helped create online sites where learning could happen:

André Boulay

André Boulay is one of the most influential yoyoers in the English-speaking world. He's taught countless people how to yoyo, and he did it all from his office without meeting them. Well, not entirely. He's done plenty of in-person teaching at his store, the A2Z Science & Learning Store. Still, the vast majority who have learned from him did so by watching videos.

He started yoyoexpert.com in 2004. When he launched the site, he represented YoYoJam, a top brand at the time. His signature yoyo, "The Dark Magic," became a staple in a generation of yoyoers' collections. He got started before YouTube became well known. He is one of the first to take yoyo instruction to streaming video. I got my start watching his tutorials.

"You have to start with a really strong sleeper" was a constant refrain from my computer speakers. He set the bar for creating video tutorials. He broke down tricks in a detailed and well thought out way that made learning easy. He shares a little of his story:

> I started mastermagic.net as a source for tutorials in 2004, with the launch of the Dark Magic 2. I shot basic lessons with basic video and broke those into steps. I spelled it out with the step numbers overlaid on the video itself as it progressed. It was definitely rough around the edges, but people managed to learn from them. I taught yoyo classes in person three days a week at A2Z Science & Learning Store and tried to do the same online. The Dark Magic had just been released, so part of it was excitement to show off the yoyo itself in the video. Of course, teaching was the main priority. I ran YoYoJam's team at the time and getting new people into the sport sat at the front of my motivations.
>
> The original tutorials on mastermagic.net were always my original idea. Around 2006, some local filmmakers looking for people to work with approached me. The website they were shooting for was called Expert Village. Their goal was to build a huge database of lessons. Which is definitely what they did. They didn't pay me much for the filming—it was more about getting your name out there and I thought it a fun idea. Little planning or preparation went into the videos. Most of them were single takes with no editing, since that was Expert Village's style at the time. YouTube hadn't taken off yet, so I had a hard time envisioning many actually learning from streaming video.
>
> I worried they would have been too difficult to learn from. However, after release on Expert Village's website, I received a substantial amount of comments and feedback. People asked about help on tricks and tips on yoyos and maintenance. I recognized that the videos on Expert Village's website were not well organized. I put effort into building a new site focused on community and teaching. This is how YoYoExpert started. We organized the videos to provide levels and building blocks. We built the community around the forum.

I asked André how he went from wanting to teach yoyo to heading one of the world's largest online retail stores.

My original intention wasn't about selling yoyos but making tutorials we could film and sell. I needed money to kickstart the idea, so I decided to sell some yoyos. It was natural for us, as things progressed, to continue with sales...I love everything yoyo and trying to showcase this to a customer is what makes the experience special. This is the excitement I enjoyed while working with YoYoJam.

André continues to inspire new throwers with his work. He puts a lot of work into curating the products offered at yoyoexpert.com, making sure each one has a story to tell. It's easy to throw together an online store. Creating an experience that generates return customers means understanding the hobby. André does that well. Despite his business success, he still loves to play with yoyos.

Brett Grimes

In 2009 when I began to yoyo, most of the phones on the market still had a physical keyboard, a tiny screen, and terrible cameras. Facebook and YouTube were still new, and Instagram didn't exist. Someone shooting high quality videos in super slow-motion stood out. Brett stepped back from yoyo a few years ago (he doesn't currently own a yoyo!) but has fond memories of the yoyo community.

High Speed YoYo came about when I first saw a video by a thrower in Russia named Fedya. He was on Team One Drop and had this cool camera that slowed things down so you could see everything in great detail. I fell in love with it, so I contacted him. He told me the make and model of the camera he used, and I saved and purchased one. It wasn't so much for a website, I just thought it looked cool. The website came a while after that. It was a place for a few of us Ohio throwers to come together and share what we were already doing. Chris Rhoads wrote reviews in the forums anyways, and I already made tutorials. I asked everyone, and we came up with highspeedyoyo.com.

I started making videos as a way to film my progress. I have always been a helpful person online and in real life. As I got better, I decided to try to film some tutorials myself and share them. It just snowballed from there! Many people liked me because I was them, so to speak. I wasn't some yoyo master, just an average guy, approachable, like most of the viewers. To this day I don't know why people followed me, but it was a great time in my life.

There were so many good times that went into High Speed YoYo and YouTube. When Jacob Gross and I first started G Squared Yoyos, every time we filmed something it was usually constant laughter. All the funny stuff happened behind the scenes, all the mistakes and screw ups.

High Speed YoYo is still available and is an excellent resource for tutorials. It's fun to scroll through old reviews of yoyos and see how design has changed.

Rethink Yoyo

Early in my yoyo career (around 2010), there were a few places to go to find quality tutorials. Rethinkyoyo.com was one of the best. Multiple angles, great descriptions, and an index of similar tricks made this site fantastic for learning. Kyle Vegh started it to provide something he felt was lacking in the yoyo world.

I picked up my first yoyo at a young age. It was a gift from my grandmother: a Playmaxx Turbo Bumblebee. I remember having to stand on a step stool to use it (I guess my parents didn't know about cutting string to length, ha-ha!). Around my twelfth birthday I started yoyoing a lot. I got a new yoyo (I can't remember which one it was, but it may have been a Yomega Raider) and trick book.

I became hooked because it was something I was finally better at than my older brother. I wasn't a quick learner, but that just made learning tricks more satisfying. When I started landing the 'Trapeze' trick consistently, my confidence soared. I started to believe I could do anything I set my mind to. I learned most everything in the trick book, and moved to a bigger trick book, then to DVDs, then to forums and YouTube.

I asked Kyle how he went from learning everything he could to sharing it. He explained:

I started rethinkyoyo.com when I found myself frustrated with the quality and depth of the available tutorials. Learning isn't easy to begin with. That difficulty is furthered when teachers don't take the time to shoot a proper angle of an element or explain a maneuver. My goal was to create tutorials with painstaking detail so that viewers would have every variable on their side. I grabbed my mom's digital camera and a rickety, partially broken tripod. I set up in my bedroom in front of pinkish window blinds and started shooting videos.

I made 30 basic tutorials before uploading. At the time, the yoyo community was a great place to take on an endeavor like this. The hobby was full of amateurs sharing content.

The community continues to pour out positivity when people share their content. I asked Kyle what kept him going once he figured how much work went into providing a free service for the community.

First, I loved the community. I could not believe how kind, welcoming, supportive, and thankful the people who came across rethinkyoyo.com were. Many would write in through the website to express thanks, to ask questions, or just to talk. Several became good email friends.

Second, I had a source of identity. In my real-life circles, I was known as the dude with the yoyo, and rethinkyoyo.com contributed to that (for better or for worse, ha-ha).

Third, rethinkyoyo.com allowed my hobby to support itself. I had four sponsors at different times, all supplying me either with yoyos or better sources. For a kid who would have done this for free, it was pretty cool. All these points are illustrated in one event. I hosted a tutorial contest through the site for a couple years. Players from around the world submitted a crazy number of tutorials. Tons of sponsors contributed prizes for the winners.

I remember learning some great tricks from the tutorials that came out of those contests! Rethinkyoyo.com is still around, but hasn't been updated in years. I asked what changed in Kyle's life.

I grew older. Honestly, it's sort of lame to admit. When I started rethinkyoyo.com, I was going through the awkward years where friends can be scarce. In college, I formed new friendships and met the girl who would later become my wife. Sadly, practicing yoyo stopped being a priority. I no longer wanted to shoot videos and spend massive amounts of hours editing footage by myself.

I still sometimes allow myself to dream about making videos again, but life's responsibilities get in the way. That might be better for the community. It's fitting to know there is not just one person or group putting out learning content. Instead it seems like there are a lot of grassroots content uploaders. Everyone contributes their unique brand of the shared hobby.

That's how life goes in a niche hobby. People drift in and out. Twenty years ago, every moment that wasn't absorbed by my university degree revolved around music. I was writing and recording music, playing in a band. I never thought that would change. Now I pick up a guitar on occasion and fiddle around. This new hobby/career of writing may one day eclipse yoyo. Life is long and full of adventures.

Mr. Matio

Youtuber "Mr. Matio" fills a different niche than most other yoyo teachers. Instead of teaching beginners, he makes tutorials for seasoned veterans. He deconstructs tricks by watching videos of top-level competitors winning contests. Few people have the patience and skill to do this. I know I don't!

I started making tutorials after I had been yoyoing for few years already. By that time, I was able to learn a few tricks from some of my favorite players.

When I started with yoyoing, I wanted to do tricks that impressed me while watching World Yoyo Contest freestyles. At that time, I really liked Japanese yoyoers like Hiroyuki Suzuki, Tatsuya Fujisaka, and Takahiro Iizuka. The trick I really wanted to learn was the fastest combo from Hiroyuki Suzuki. I learned that trick and posted a video of me practicing it and everyone seemed to want a tutorial how to do it.

Since then, I started to post a few tutorials per year. As for why I do it? It's a hobby, and it's nice to help players that are not beginners anymore. To allow them to learn a trick from their favorite yoyo player. The best part is seeing someone at a yoyo contest doing a trick I made a tutorial to.

At EYYC 2017 I met Evan Nagao, who later became World Champion, and I wanted to make a trick videoclip with him. I started chatting with him and learned he actually knew my video tutorials and that he learned some tricks from them. When he won Worlds in 2018, I later recognized the trick he mentioned to me in his winning freestyle. Moments like that makes the time spent with making tutorials worthwhile."

I asked him if he makes any money from his tutorials.

I also monetize videos on YouTube, but yoyoing seems to be a poor niche for advertisement. I don't have many views per month, since I don't upload new videos that often and I make tutorials for more advanced players. I also often get demonetized because of music and many viewers come from countries with very low ad fees. It is usually around 20-25 USD per month for 30 000 views.

That's not much, but it's about what I'd expect. My next question was how he chooses which tricks to learn.

I choose tricks I like and those that I feel I have a chance of learning. I prefer tricks where I can find multiple videos and angles. Sometimes I get requests for tricks from viewers, but I always choose tricks myself. It's tedious trial and error. I watch in slow motion, frame by frame. It takes me a lot of time; I am not learning tricks quickly. It takes multiple days, sometimes weeks learning a trick.

I want to share a fun thought I had a while ago. I might have contributed to populariz[ing] the term 'speed combo.' This term wasn't used commonly before. When you search the term 'yoyo speed combo' on YouTube and sort results by date, the oldest entries are some of my first tutorials to 'speed combos.'

I wanted to name the video where I was teaching the fastest combo from Hiroyuki Suzuki. I only came up with the name 'speed combo' since I am not a native English speaker. Yuuki Spencer's winning freestyle of the World Yoyo Contest 2007 where he used the 'Speed song' inspired me.

I've tried learning a few tricks from Mr. Matio's tutorials. They are very well crafted, but I lack the patience. When I try to learn tricks from videos, I tend to get far enough that I learn a new element, then go off and make my own trick with it. But many yoyoers out there learn everything he releases and clamour for more.

Yoyotricks.com

(picture – I wanna learn to yoyo. There's an app for that)

Adam Bottigilia came at teaching from a different angle than André Boulay of yoyoexpert.com. His goal from the outset was to create a viable business—a way to bring in some income while sharing his passion with kids and drawing them into the hobby he loves so much.

The team at YoYoTricks push the visionary edge. They created the first yoyo tutorial cell phone app. I film tutorials with a cell phone camera and simple editing software. YoYoTricks combines high-quality video and detailed editing to produce the best quality tutorials I've seen. They offer multiple angles, close-ups, slow-motion break downs, and a detailed verbal explanation for every trick.

Adam set up the YoYoTricks website like a video game. You log in, and every time you learn a trick you check it off and gain "Experience Points" towards higher ranks. They've refined what André, Kyle, and others like him started. I've had the privilege of chatting with Adam a few times now. I asked how he got started down this path.

> For me yoyoing was always more of a side hustle while I worked my way through school. I started college at the same time the yoyo craze hit in the late 90s. I had connected to several of the big yoyo companies by sending VHS tapes of my tricks through the mail. When things started to go global, the Duncan Yoyo Company invited me to join their team. Yomega wanted to make me the face of their brand (they later chose Ooch for this honor).
>
> Yomega wanted me to quit school to work for them full time, which I was unwilling to do. Later that same year (1997) Peter Fish from Australia needed a player for a small promotion in the UK. He was happy to work around my school schedule, so I gladly obliged. He also flew me to the New York toy fair the next year, where I had a picture taken for the short-lived yoyo magazine Fiend.
>
> After I finished my undergraduate work I was working on my Master's degree in Chicago when I recorded my first yoyo tutorial series. I paid for almost half of my education by street performing on the weekends. One hundred tricks in total. I built the videos into an interactive CD-ROM I programmed myself. I couldn't get the audio right, so I superimposed text instructions on the video. I called it 'No Frills, Just Yo!' I believe it was the largest collection of tricks available at the time (2002), with the possible exception of the 'Sector_Y' website.
>
> I sold the CDs, which I burned one-at-a-time on my computer, at King's Yomen shows for an additional $5 over the cost of a yoyo. I made a second series of videos a few years later (with

audio this time!) and put them onto a DVD which we also sold at shows. After I finished my Master's, I spent a few years at a software company learning web development.

Peter Fish contacted me again in 2009 about building a tutorial website to promote his new line of yoyos. By that time, I had a lot of experience to draw upon. Peter planned to do a one-year promotion for his yoyos. What he wanted from me was a website teaching 20 tricks using the yoyos. I told him I would do a lot more than 20 tricks if I could have ownership of the website after the one-year promotion. He agreed. So began yoyotricks.com.

At the time I believed I could create the best yoyo tutorial website in the world. I also hoped it would become a standalone business, a back-up in case my other plans fell through. At the very least it would be a good resource for the kids getting yoyos at our shows.

That is quite the unique adventure! It was really neat learning his history. Prior to this, I just thought he was a guy who started making tutorials. Adam and his team have brought a stream of new yoyoers into the hobby and continue to build the sport.

Patrick Dressel

Patrick Dressel (aka Hobbygod) is another yoyoer who has found a passion for teaching. It's neat finding people in this community who have shared a similar path in life. Patrick is a prime example of the blend of interests that yoyoers share.

I like tutorials because I enjoy helping people. I'm finishing up college to become a teacher this semester. Tutorials seemed like a solid way to blend two of my passions/talents together. A great way for me to help and interact with yoyo players of different skill levels.

Where Kyle of rethinkyoyo.com focused on high-quality multi-angle tutorials, Patrick uses a similar style to me—simple instructions which fit our current world of high-output, fast consumption.

It doesn't take much camera equipment or editing software. I use my phone and sometimes a phone holder for a first-person view. People can get the satisfaction of learning a new trick or hearing some different tips/ideas for a trick that might end up clicking for them. It's also a good way to share new ideas with people that are newer to the yoyo community.

I also enjoy creating tutorials that are more personal and descriptive than your typical one to two minute slow motion tutorials. I'm following that trend a little now because school is eating up most of my time, but when I can I enjoy making longer tutorials. I prefer my tutorials to be more of a discussion. Players feel more comfortable reaching out to me for more help if something doesn't click for them.

That's one of the joys of being a teacher: those connections with other yoyoers. It's a great feeling to know you've added a bit of joy to someone's life.

These are just a few examples of the available resources for learning. Kyle spoke of grassroots content uploaders—an apt description. If you visit Instagram and search for "#trickcircle," you'll find hundreds of people sharing what they've learned. Many take the time to guide others around the mistakes they made while learning.

I've scratched the surface of the long list of teachers in this community. Patrick and Brett are great examples of grassroots teaching. Dale offers a top-down approach as the person bringing yoyo to kids—kids who grow up to find the online community. Adam and André both teach as part of their business, bringing in customers that find their tutorials and stick around to shop. There are dozens, if not hundreds, of others on social media or at your local yoyo club who are teaching the next generations the joy of yoyo. There are so many creative yoyoers out there that you could spend a lifetime learning tricks.

Chapter 8: The Community Leader

Leadership is a difficult skill to master. One student in my Grade 2 class this year has the intelligence and personality to be an effective leader. When you are seven years old, however, it's hard to understand what leadership looks like. They get accused of being "bossy" by other students. What's the difference between leadership and "being bossy"? Being bossy goes with telling people what to do because you want them to do it.

Leadership is figuring out what people need or want and then guiding them to that goal. It's the difference between "Pick up that piece of paper" and "Would you like to help keep our space tidy by picking up that piece of paper?" One is an order, the other a guiding suggestion.

In the yoyo community, leadership takes many forms. Some of us are out there in public yoyoing and catching the eye of potential new yoyoers. These leaders carry a beginner yoyo around for curious folks to try. Others are teaching - in schools, on YouTube, or at contests. The best of our champions lead by example, showing how hard work and perseverance pay off. Moderators in social media groups are important; they keep things safe and on track. Some individuals organize contests, start yoyo clubs, and try out new ways to share the love of yoyo.

I love seeing yoyoers find leadership positions, especially the ones who don't even think of themselves as influential. Anyone who throws a spare yoyo in their bag in case they meet someone curious is a community leader. People who attend yoyo club regularly help drive the sport forward.

Bradly Twitty is exactly that person. He says:

> I don't consider myself a leader. I don't think I've been in the game long enough for that status. But I work to grow the yoyo community around me in Alabama (which is super small). I'm constantly yoyoing in public, catching the eyes of adults and children of all ages and sharing information with anyone who shows interest. I may not make videos or post much on Instagram, but I'm out there in the streets, advocating yoyos and trying to share the love.

Connor Scholten has the right attitude when it comes to leadership:

> I do it because I feel good showing others the secrets I have found in yoyoing. I share so others can listen and help people succeed.

That's leadership. Find something that makes you happy, then step up and show others the path to that same feeling.

Wayne Ngan

I've known Wayne Ngan for almost a decade. Canada is one of the largest countries in the world, but our population is tiny—especially when you start counting yoyoers! Wayne was one of the founding members of the Vancouver Yoyo Club until he moved to the other end of the country. He's now a key player in the Toronto yoyo scene. He runs the Eastern Canadian Regional Contest and the Canadian National Championship every other year. I asked him to share the story of how he found his way into the contest organizer role. He explains:

> I started hanging out with the Toronto Yoyo Club back in 2009 when I moved to Toronto. The club was already pretty well established. I found them through the YoYoNation forums, so

I already knew the people there before I moved there. By an awesome coincidence, their yoyo meets happened a five-minute walk away from my house and work. On a weekend afternoon (and I was usually free on weekends) yoyo club for me was just stepping out of my door with yoyo in hand.

In a big city with a decent sized yoyo club, it makes perfect sense to have a yoyo contest in Toronto. I watched Canadian contests happening on the opposite side of the country for years. I decided it was time to 'be the change you want to see.' Running a contest is challenging on multiple levels. There is the material challenge (the logistics). You go through your list of things to do—venue, sponsors, judges, etc. Then there are mental challenges. You keep asking yourself, have I done everything I could? What could still go wrong? What if no one comes? The first time I ran a contest I didn't know these answers, and I lost a lot of sleep over it. I felt super fortunate that I had a lot of local support from the yoyo club and sponsors. Things went well enough to make regional and national contests sustainable.

Despite the success of the first contest, in hindsight so many things didn't go as I thought. There were so many lessons learned. I've run a few regionals and nationals now. Every year the work is still there, the unknowns are still unknowns, but I've learned to deal with them. I don't feel as nervous as before. Being a software developer myself helps. The software that I used for contests— the registration, music, judging systems—all improve every year. They are automatic enough that using them now is just a matter of clicking a few buttons. Looking back, I am impressed that I managed to do all those things by hand for the first time!

As people grow older, especially with young adult yoyoers, life priorities change, and sometimes yoyo club moves down the list a bit. Over 10 years—from 2009 when I first joined to present day 2019—the group who make up the yoyo club are almost entirely different! Old regulars fade away, new faces appear. The yoyo club stayed in this 'equilibrium' for 10 years.

We never seemed to run out of new people. I guess this is an advantage of being Toronto with a few million people living in it. Once you set up some kind of social media presence, people just find it. If you live in a major metropolitan area, chances are there are plenty of yoyoers around you. You need only go find them!

I have great respect for Wayne. When I run Canadian Nationals, it's a bit chaotic. I'm good at people, but systems are my weak spot. So, over the years, I've built a team of parents and volunteers. Wayne does the same in Toronto, but I suspect he handles a lot more than I do. If you've ever attended a yoyo contest, track down the organizer—not the day after the contest, but a few months later. A simple "I enjoyed the contest, thanks again," goes a long way. No one is making money organizing yoyo contests. It's a service for a hobby we are passionate about.

Jim-E Pendall

Jim-E Pendall is one of the key people in yoyo—the people who make local clubs happen. For the better part of a decade I was the person who showed up every week club to make sure yoyo club happens. It's a big commitment. It pays off in community growth and sheer joy as each new person finds the club and starts a new chapter of their lives. Jim-E shares:

I am the creator/organizer of Throw Life Away Yoyo Club in Huntsville, Alabama. Once I saw my daughter begin to take interest in yoyo, I noticed her friends were also intrigued by it. I wanted our club to be as a haven not only to yoyo [and] learn to yoyo, but [also] just to come and feel involved as a community.

I wanted to seek and find others who not only enjoyed the recreational aspect, but those who also appreciated yoyo as a culture within itself. There's still a lot to cultivate and conceptualize within different areas of play.

Right now I want to direct my effort toward community and civic focuses. Many kids would love to go, some who don't even own a yoyo, or who just need a little support. Within the next couple of years, I hope I can reach outward and bring more people into yoyo. To give them something that can be a positive impact in their lives like it has mine.

Usually I'll arrange meet ups at the library or Big Spring Park. I always have extra yoyos with me and encourage people of all ages to come play. I'm finding people are fascinated. Yoyo brings up memories of their youth. People always stop and take interest—they share stories of how they had this kind or that kind of yoyo as a kid. I'm always hoping to further grow our club here and offer any resources I can. We welcome anyone local, parents, kids, friends of my daughter. Yoyo is creative and fun, and we are always hoping for more people to come by.

Yeti B.

Yeti B. is very much a behind-the-scenes leader. He's one of the grownups of the yoyo world, helping guide the younger yoyoers. He is also training to be one of the heroes of the yoyo world—the judges. They are often maligned for imperfection in a subjective sport. Yet without them, contests wouldn't happen.

In a weird way, I always end up being the 'Dad' with a full crew of misfits (shout out to Ohyesyo and Freshly Dirty). I am well known because of my willingness to let people use my yoyos. I'm a collector and an inquisitive guy. Manufacturers and company owners know I'm always looking for the next new and upcoming thing. Sometimes I get lucky and receive promos to show off at events. I feel this role of Dad is important, as a lot of yoyo players need a voice of reason. Many players gravitate to the yoyo for the mental release. Bad ideas can sometimes surface in a group setting. I don't tell people how to live their lives. I make sure everyone is safe, in a good place, mentally, and ready to hit the stage when competing.

Yoyo is a sport that attracts all sorts. Yet as we'll see later in the book, many of us struggle emotionally, especially at big gatherings. People like Yeti who can keep things chill help make yoyo fun.

Josh Prokay

Josh Prokay is one of those critical people in the internet age—someone willing to put in the time and put up with the complaints that come along with moderating a forum. Most people in the yoyo community are honest and well-intentioned. Sometimes people make mistakes or bad decisions. Sometimes they need guidance to follow the community standards. Very rarely, someone needs to be removed. Josh's task is a tightrope of keeping things safe and inclusive. He says:

> I took on the role of moderator in a peculiar way. Before I was a moderator, there was a scammer that took advantage of several people. Myself included. I reached out to his mom in an attempt to find a resolution. Long story short, I made a thread for people to tell me about their specific situation with this scammer. I said something to the effect of 'No witch hunts or bashing, or I will delete your comment.' I found out I couldn't delete comments unless I was a moderator. Tucker let me know and he made me a moderator so I could keep control of that thread. After a few days, he messaged me back and told me he wanted to keep me because it seemed I knew what I was doing. Pro tip: I didn't.

> I kept the role because I wanted to help the yoyo community in any way I could. It's the most supportive and interesting group I've ever had the pleasure of being a member of. I had been around the community for almost 10 years at that point and was well aware of what needed doing while dealing with scammers.

> I've even been on the other end when I was young and agreed to deals without having the means to ship. It's difficult getting to the post office when you're 13 (ha-ha). I understand that sometimes scamming is a misunderstanding, or a snowball effect of unfortunate situations. Most people deserve a second chance, or a way to right their wrongs. I like to help people.

You would think it's a thankless job, but it's not. One of the most mind-blowing things is people approaching me at contests and thanking me for being a moderator. Evan Nagao and Colin Beckford were among them. I was blown away that simply moderating a Facebook group was enough to have people introducing themselves and thanking me. I'm not a doctor, firefighter, or teacher, so it seems silly to me. Maybe it's just a good icebreaker?

People both online and in person have been super nice and I appreciate it whether I believe it's warranted. Some people are grateful because I listened to them vent about their day for a few minutes. Things like that prove how supportive and amazing this community can be. I was pretty intimidated by being a moderator in the beginning. They're often the most criticized and tainted, but it's been the exact opposite.

Leadership is natural for some people, learnable for others. Until you take a chance, step up and try, you never know! If there aren't any yoyoers in your area, this might be your chance. Buy a half dozen inexpensive yoyos and start showing up in a public place once a week and teaching beginners. You may find you shine!

Josh continues to do a fantastic job of keeping the Facebook group "Yoyo BST & Talk" civilized. It's the biggest, most active yoyo group Facebook, so what he does is appreciated!

Ross Levine

In the 1990s, it was more common to find yoyos in stores, with yoyo pros running classes. Big brands would regularly partner with local stores to host their touring yoyo pros. The times have changed, and stores are less likely to take a risk on a $60 competition yoyo than they used to on a $12 yoyo. Ross Levine shares a memory of a community leader who built a small community of players.

I grew up in Redondo beach where there was a kite shop that sold yoyos and held classes. A friend of mine named Julian and I would go and hang out there every Saturday for hours. The teacher and shop attendant was named Yoshi. He worked there most of the afternoon, so if we stayed past the end of the official class time, we'd get a bunch of free learning time. It was a tiny shop with hardly any customers. I imagine Yoshi tolerated us staying so long since we were, at worst, company that he could yoyo with.

We went to those classes every Saturday for years and in that time, we watched regulars come and go. People learned to start yoyoing and grew to love yoyoing. Some of the more notable regulars that I saw were Grant Johnson, Alex Hattori, Anthony Rojas, and Alex Kim (owner of Recreational Revolution). I'm pretty sure Yoshi taught or at least heavily influenced players such as Alex Hattori, Grant Johnson, and Patrick Borgerding. Yoshi also did a ton of work with YoYoJam. He judged countless contests in Southern California and elsewhere. Plus Yoshi is an incredible yoyoer himself. I recommend you do yourself a favor and look up some of his 2a Nationals' freestyles.

The kite shop isn't selling yoyos anymore, but Yoshi still teaches and inspires generations of yoyoers. His most recent notable student, Justin Dauer, just got sponsored by Duncan. Yoshi is, in my mind, what every yoyoer should be. He's someone that teaches anyone who wants to learn and gives to the community with no expectations.

Shay Oliver

Shay is a natural leader, the kind that gets so excited that it's infectious. You need not be a pro to be a leader. Shay is learning with the rest of us and inspires from a place of equality.

I dipped my toes in the yoyo water first in the 90s, with a Yomega Brain. I gave up because of the combination of auto-clutch design (too many smacked fingers) and the lack of learning materials. Then in 2014, the NED show came to my niece's school and thinking it was a fundraiser I ended up with a yoyo. Throwing appealed to me because I can quantify my progress. I can add up the tricks I know; every trick is a victory, a moment of pride! That validation, that feeling of pride, has been a rare thing in my life. It makes the frustration of uncountable misses worth it!

Today, I feel like a seasoned thrower and, since I am over 30, an ancient! I focus less on the hype and excitement and more into the atmosphere of throwing. When I throw it is mostly to find inner peace. There is something amazing about the inner balance a simple toy provides me.

The focus and the art of manipulating the strings allows the world to fade away. Being a thrower is about being part of the community. I am a loner by nature. I am socially awkward and live a non-heteronormative life. I am non-binary (in fact some may know me by my old name Stephanie Honeycutt). This puts me on the fringe of society. Despite these things, or because of it, I have found a place in this open and 'come as you are' community.

I have never met one group of people who, as a whole, were so kind and generous with their time, their knowledge, with their stuff. The traveling mystery box called 'Throw it Forward' seemed a great way to give back to the community. I was fortunate that I had a place on the Rain City Skills team for a while, where I focused on helping the community through the

Facebook group 'Mr. Yoyothrower's Minions.' I have found a place of welcome and a place of comfort in the yoyo world. A place where I don't feel so out of sorts. I am proud to be a Thrower!

One of Shay's contributions to the yoyo world is the "Throw it Forward" program mentioned above. Shay created a program to give people a chance to try new yoyos without spending a fortune. They explain:

I started ['Throw it Forward'] for a couple reasons. I wanted to find a use for a couple yoyos I had that didn't hold enough value to be worth selling. Not to mention the chance to try out as many yoyos as I could! My small collection needed refreshing, I wanted to swap out the ones I didn't care for. I had already learned that the images, specifications, and reviews on a yoyo only tell you so much. You have to play with it to see if it fits you. So I took a chance.

The basic concept is the box has three yoyos in it and small gifts (think of a stocking at Christmas). I posted on the Facebook BST group and to my astonishment 27 people signed up!

The whole experience was incredible and chaotic. I learned once again that people don't read instructions. I also had a fun time figuring out the US postal system. It took over three months to circulate, and almost everyone had questions. Some asked me if all the gifts were for them, others were unsure what to take.

The first box was an experiment. I set it up so I was taking most of the risk. Others would only 'lose' on participating if there was nothing wanted in the box.

Shay has crafted a detailed set of rules for the people taking part in the program. The basic framework is this:

1. The box will include three yoyos and a small 'goodie bag.'

2. Each person will receive the box and get to keep one yoyo and the goodie bag.

3. They replace it with a yoyo from their collection, and a new goodie bag for the next person, then ship to them.

4. The value of the yoyos is decided at the beginning [at one point she was running multiple value levels]. This way each person swaps out a throw roughly equal in value."

Shay shares how the program has evolved over time:

No surprise, it turned into far more work than expected! Later, boxes followed with a goal of doing one every month. I added stricter guidelines and some of the mystery [was] abandoned. I limited the boxes to 15 participants and re-categorized to contain yoyos of a certain retail price range.

After the first two, I had to get volunteers to help start boxes. This gave me some anxiety; I didn't want someone else getting ripped off. And someone did. Turns out the way I had constructed the guidelines were too vague. I did my best to make it up to the volunteer.

A group of volunteers worked as a sounding board to help make sure everything was clear. The last couple of boxes circulated without any trouble or disappointment.

I tried something similar with Rain City Skills yoyos. Twice in fact. Both times, the box didn't make it past the second person (One box came back). People's lives are full, and it's hard to stay on top of everything that's happening. In both cases, people were too busy to meet their commitments. Shay plans to continue the program, although the once-a-month timeline turned out to be way too much work. Either way, it's a neat idea, and a great way around the challenge of getting your hands on a yoyo before buying it!

Luckey Yulin Li

Luckey Li is a world-class yoyoer who has been developing his expertise for 10 years. He started yoyoing about the same time as I did and joined the Vancouver Yoyo Club not long after. He's worked hard to hone his skills over the years and is a well-known competitor the world over. We worked together for a few years when I was the North American manager of Chinese yoyo brand King Yo Star. Luckey helped with translation and promotion.

He's a truly world class yoyoer. He's won the Canadian Championships four times, as well as contests around the world (USA, Europe, Japan, China). I had a conversation with him many years ago about the lack of a proper contest system in China. At the time, a big toy company organized the event, and it wasn't the same as contests elsewhere. In

2019, he worked with other Chinese yoyoers to create the Chinese Yoyo Association. They organized the first player-run Chinese National Contest.

Luckey is also a yoyo designer and has worked with a few brands designing great throws. He saw that the market didn't have a high-quality, reasonably priced accessories company. So, he started one called Sochi that has been a rousing success. I asked him to talk a bit about the yoyo scene in China and the challenges of running a National contest there.

In China, the National Contest used to be run every year by a big yoyo brand, Auldey. They planned to stop running it, so I saw a chance to give back to the community. I had many contacts with Chinese yoyo business so I thought I could do it. Jeyo Wang, the head judge of the China National Contest and a World Contest judge, helped ensure the contest followed the rules. It was my first time running a contest with over 200 people, so I was nervous! It's difficult to run a contest in China. There are too many people!

The contest was two days long and something always went wrong. For example: A couple days before the contest, I realized I forgot to order clickers for the contest. I ordered some, but they didn't come in time. One judge had enough clickers, so it was OK.

After the first day, I realized the stage was clear like glass, so it reflected the light. This made it hard for the judges and the audience to see the yoyo string. People still did a perfect routine, so I think it was OK, but I wanted competitors to have a good experience.

I was exhausted the whole time because there were so many jobs to do. A 4am alarm each day woke me to set up the venue. I only slept six hours during the whole event! Afterwards, I never wanted to run a contest again. But when I got back to Vancouver and posted the videos people had nice things to say. So I will do it again.

Next year Auldey will work with the Chinese Yoyo Association and help pay for the contest. We will make it an even better contest!

I was curious how the yoyo scene in China was different from in North

America. The population is so much larger and the culture different. Luckey explains:

> The culture is different. Players don't complain about judges or anything. Chinese judges are very good, they really know the rules and how to score tricks correctly. The contests are different. American contests are like a party, but Chinese contests are more serious. Japan and the US have very good systems for the yoyo contests. I tried to create my own system like the AYYA and JYYL, but it didn't work well. We cannot handle all the contests that happen in China.
>
> Contests in China usually have high budgets and are very professionally run events. Contests are often run by people who aren't yoyoers, but businesses that sell yoyos. So they don't know as much about the sport. I suspect China has the biggest yoyo market because China has Taobao. It's like Amazon but a lot bigger.
>
> People in China buy a lot of yoyos. They aren't all yoyoers, people buy yoyos for gifts for kids' birthdays. Cheap yoyos can sell very well, so a lot of companies that aren't yoyo players sell yoyos. It is easy and cheap to make yoyos. You don't have to spend a lot of money to create a brand, just give some money to the factory and they will give you a design.
>
> Chinese players get a good chance to get high-quality yoyos, but it means you cannot charge a high price. Well, except for Japanese yoyos. Chinese people like to buy Japanese yoyos, but they don't like American yoyos as much. Powerful yoyos that are very good for contest play sell well. People in China do not think Chinese yoyos are worth a high price. They think yoyos from outside China are better. This isn't true, you can get good quality yoyos in China.

Yoyo spans cultures and continents. The Chinese yoyo scene reflects the culture there. However, yoyoers are still yoyoers. If you attend a World Yoyo Contest, you'll spot folks from all over the world hanging out and sharing tricks, even if they lack a shared language. I have friends all over the world that I chat to about yoyos and life. Contest structures and cultural differences aside, a yoyo is a yoyo. We have that in common, and it's a fantastic starting place.

Competitors are a fascinating group of yoyoers. They are often shy, content to spend hours alone with their yoyo. Those same people get up on stage in front of hundreds of people and showcase their skills for the world to see. Many are friendly and more than happy to share but are not the outgoing public figures needed to help the sport grow.

Then we have players like Gentry Stein and Evan Nagao—two World Champions who are comfortable in the spotlight and passionate about their roles as yoyo ambassadors.

Gentry Stein

Gentry is one of the few yoyoers to win the title of World Champion more than once. He has traveled the world promoting yoyo. He teaches every chance he gets, encourages young yoyoers, and shows the world that yoyo is cool. He shares:

> As a World Champion I am an ambassador. I have traveled to promote yoyo in over 15 different countries. I've been featured on television shows and starred in the music video for the single 'Strings' by Baby Raptors. I won the US Nationals with a $16 YoyoFactory Replay.
>
> My life is filled with amazing experiences, all of which stemmed from this passion. My goal of changing what the public sees as possible with a yoyo continues. I'm incredibly excited to keep pushing the boundaries of creation and inspiring others to follow their passion.

I love that he won a title with a beginner-friendly yoyo. He showed the world that you need not spend a fortune to be a yoyo champion.

Evan Nagao

Evan Nagao is a performer as much as he is a competitor. His stage presence and showmanship are beyond most other yoyoers. What's even more impressive is his positivity and enthusiasm. He loves yoyoing and is great at encouraging others to join in the fun. He promotes the sport every chance he gets. His World Championship routine even made the front page of Reddit—thus introducing many, many new people to the amazing sport of yoyo. He says:

> As one of the top competitors on the scene, it's impossible to not have some level of influence. As someone in this position it's always important to realize the responsibility that comes with it. I try my best to create peace within the community. I do what I can to help keep our culture wholesome and enjoyable.
>
> I believe part of winning big titles comes with a responsibility to push yoyoing forward. If I win a big contest, and do nothing to grow the sport, I haven't fulfilled my responsibilities as the champion. I feel, as the US National Yoyo Champion, [it's my job] to do press releases and appear on large media outlets to spread the word. There will only be one champion each year, so if the opportunity to grow yoyoing isn't taken, then it's wasted.

Role models are the best advertiser for anything. Leadership comes in all forms, and we need high-profile ambassadors to draw in new yoyoers. From there, the Teachers step in and guide these new recruits on their path.

Leadership is a funny thing. Humans have an innate need to be acknowledged and accepted by our groups. We want replies to our posts, "likes" on our videos, and friends to hang out with at clubs and contests. For the wonderful few leaders in our communities, this means stepping out and making sure people are included—making sure there are events, clubs, and online spaces to join and have a good time. It's not always easy, but it is rewarding. I'm grateful to have had opportunities to help people find and get involved with yoyo.

Chapter 9: The Performer

There have been times in recent North American history where one could make a living off yoyos. The 1940s-1960s saw a small army of yoyo demonstrators touring America. In the 1990s, traveling yoyo demonstrators spearheaded another great yoyo boom. One of the side effects of the advancement of yoyo technology is that such a big "boom" won't likely come again. High cost/low profit yoyos mean travelling teams of demonstrators are too expensive. Key demographics (kids and teens) live in a world of social media. Television advertising isn't effective for targeting them.

The double-edged sword of YouTube means the bar for entry is higher, but the people who do get into yoyo are dedicated. Yoyo tricks are far more intimidating than they used to be. You can watch someone "Rock the Baby" and conceive of learning that trick. What modern yoyo pros do looks like magic. The focus used to be mastering a dozen tricks for the standard contest when the yoyo man came to town. Now the focus for many is to assemble a one to three minute contest routine. I often find myself faced with the situation where I show off my best tricks for people and it puts them off. They say, "That's way too hard, I could never do that."

Enter the yoyo performer.

Master performers like Mark Hayward, Chih-Minh Tuan, Dazzling Dave Schulte, and John Higby deliver entertainment. They use simple yoyo tricks with a twist to make the near-impossible seem simple.

The audience thinks, "My dad used to yoyo like that, maybe I should try." Each performer approaches the profession from a different angle. They share a focus on using the yoyo to entertain and tell a story. They make it approachable while keeping the magic—a skill that only a seasoned entertainer can deliver.

John Higby

My personality as a yoyoer is amplified on stage. I've always thought of the yoyo as a way to communicate with people.

John Higby is one of the few people making a full-time living as a yoyo performer. He travels the world with his wife, entertaining crowds large and small. He has held four Guinness World Records. His most recent one involved knocking coins off people's ears with a yoyo—14 in 60 seconds.

He is master of a busking style performance, common with street performers. He uses props, costumes, audience interaction, and humor. It's not unusual to see Higby throwing a yoyo on a 30-foot long string out over the heads of a crowd or riding a unicycle while "Shooting the Moon." He explains:

> A 45-minute engaging show differs from mastering a three-minute skill for a contest. I'm more a fan of comedy circus than I am of contest freestyles. I started street performing in 1992 and still enjoy it. Stage shows are my favourite, I like what you can do with good lighting and setup.

After 20+ years of performing, he's a master at it.

In 2013, John Higby was the MC at the Canadian National Championship. He delivered his world-famous stage show between competition divisions. A yoyo with a 10m long string flew out over the heads of the audience. Then, a young volunteer stood at the back of the audience holding a large butterfly net while Higby launched an offstring yoyo from the stage, across the crowd, and straight into the net. He then repeated this trick again with a smaller net, hardly bigger than the yoyo. This time, he managed to hit the edge of the net, but the yoyo stuck! He rewarded the young volunteer for their bravery with a crisp five-dollar bill. It was a masterful performance; he held the audience in the palm of his hand.

I asked him to share his favourite memory from his career as a yoyo pro.

I just did the Gong Show and gave Tommy Maitland (Mike Myers) a hand painted yoyo during the rehearsal. He totally loved it and hugged me so hard. It was surreal to be next to such a legend.

From my perspective, Higby is a legend!

Mark Hayward

Another yoyo icon from North America is 1995 World Champion Mark Hayward. He's a master of stage performance. He recently took the Guinness World Record for the longest "Walk the Dog" trick - the single most requested trick in any yoyoer's repertoire. Mark spends his life as a professional comedy entertainer, speaker, and skill toy expert.

I say "skill toy expert" because his show isn't limited to yoyo tricks. In 2014, I attended the first "Las Vegas Open" yoyo contest. This event was part of a larger event called Skillcon which featured nearly two dozen different skill events. A yoyo contest was right at home with juggling, breakdancing, dodgeball, and sign spinning. The event even had a flare bartending contest! Mark was the MC for the yoyo portion of the event, and he put on a very engaging show. He combined yoyo tricks and stunts with perfect comedic delivery to take the audience on a journey.

Mark also presented a talk at a TEDx conference on how failure builds success. He discussed how the best experiences can begin as mistakes and outright disasters. The show centered on the value of using "mistakes" to build tension in a performance. It's something I'd never considered, but it's true that a trick is all-the-more impressive if it's shown to be hard to perform.

Once I heard him explain this, I thought back to the street performers I've watched. A master juggler working up to juggling knives and fire will start the show easy with balls or scarves. They will likely drop some balls "accidentally" early in the show. Once the blades come out, there's tension. Will he drop a blade? Is his hair going to catch on fire? In the end, the success of a performance comes in part from the relief of tension. The audience rides a wave of adrenaline and shares in the performer's success.

So, what's involved in being a successful yoyo performer? The answer is hard work—really hard work. Mark shares his thoughts:

I'm definitely a performer first, but that's because it's how I make my living. I have to devote most of my time to the show and business to earn money. I love yoyoing, but if I don't learn a trick, it doesn't mean that I can't pay my bills in the same way as if I didn't get a contract or answer my emails. For competition, you must present new tricks and top-level yoyoing and do it in three minutes. As a performer, I have to present upscale entertainment. It has to be the right thing for that audience, at that moment, and in that venue.

A few new tricks are good, but it's important to do the classics that people love. I usually do an hour-long show. That's a very different process than making a three-minute competition routine.

Like John Higby, Mark focuses on what the audience needs. One of the fun parts of being a performer is the connections you make with audience members. He explains:

I love it when people come up afterwards and share their stories about yoyoing when they were younger. It's usually someone who won the local contest when they were little. At one show, I had a guy who told me he used to do some yoyoing. I talked to him, as I always do in these situations, but I didn't expect much. But he said he used to demonstrate and pulled out a scrapbook filled with articles and photos of him yoyoing.

It turned out to be Bill Cafe, one of the main demonstrators for Duncan back in the glory days of the 50s and 60s! I was astonished! He just showed up at my show! It was a blast talking with him, and then he came to Worlds that year. So cool.

Dazzling Dave Schulte

Mark and John are both stage performers—showmen. Dazzling Dave Schulte has been that and more. He started his yoyo career during the yoyo boom of the 1990s with Team High Performance. Team High Performance was a marketing organization created to bring yoyo into the mainstream by traveling the world and demonstrating. Dave reminisces:

> *When I started this gig, I was working for Team High Performance. They were based in Honolulu, Hawaii. I travelled around the world, places like Japan, Korea, France, and Australia. It was great. Then I came home and started working for myself and found I can only travel as far as someone [was] willing to pay. Over the last 15-20 years I've had more than a few cool gigs. I was back in Australia for a while. San Diego, Chicago, Las Vegas—the big areas.*

Most demonstrators from that era moved on to other passions. Dave couldn't shake the yoyo bug, and he spun it into a 20-year career by being everything yoyo to every audience. One of the hardest parts of being a professional performer is finding the work and paying the bills. He shared a laundry list of possible job types, from school gigs, birthdays, and cub scouts' events to corporate retreats and trade shows.

> *What does life as a full-time performer look like? It's incredibly busy for me during the summer. I do around seven shows a week, although that's not a show every single day. Some days I do two or three shows. Work is nonstop for me from about June 7th through August 29th. Things slow down during the school year. I do one school a week and maybe one corporate gig a month.*

> *You have to be more than good at tricks because there are tons of people who can yoyo well. Being a teacher is super important. I was a middle school teacher before I became a Yoyo Professional, so I know how to manage children. I understand how they work, react, and learn. My program is called 'The Science of Spin.' I come out and spend an entire day, sometimes two at a school. I teach the science behind spinning things, then teaching the kids how to yoyo. It's a free program, as long as they sell my yoyos.*

I started as a hobbyist in the early 1990s, and then a competitor in the late 1990s. Throughout I was a collector, and to this day I have about 2000 yoyos. I feel now, my biggest contribution to the sport is as a teacher. Before I became a full-time yoyo pro in 1998, I was a Tech Ed teacher for middle school. Teaching is in my blood. Now I just concentrate on the yoyo end of things. I excel at helping absolute beginners to master the basics."

The biggest key is that you have to love yoyos because I can tell you I'm not doing the most amazing tricks. I'm spending hours teaching kids how to throw the sleeper. That's most of my day, the basics. Of course, you must be good at performing on stage, not doing great tricks, but the ones they want to see.

Talk about a long-term strategy—teach kids to yoyo, and then they grow up and have kids who grow up to be customers! I've done a few school demo/workshop days. It's non-stop physical and mental work. Managing 20-30 kids and keeping them from smacking each other in the head with a yoyo is hard enough; doing it for class after class among a wide age range takes a masterful touch. Dave teaches all ages, but his biggest challenge has been daycares, where he's been known to entertain children as young as 18 months old!

Should you be in the position of hiring an entertainer for an event, you may be surprised at the price. "They are making how much for an hour?" When people hire me to demonstrate and teach yoyo, they are not just paying for an hour of my time. They are paying for a teaching degree and 15 years experience. They are paying for the prep and travel as well.

Entertainers need to manage a business—this means they juggle accounting, inventory, scheduling, customer service, and a mountain of business costs. All this comes out of your pay for those one-hour gigs. I briefly considered trying to build a business as a full-time entertainer. It was more than I could handle. Dave's in a position now where the job has become a little easier.

When I started this job, I was a little nervous about the gigs and where they would come from. But now that it's been my full-time job for over 20 years, I'm not worried about it. I know the shows are coming.

I guess that's the case with any entrepreneurial business. If you stick with it and do it well, you build up a list of contacts that generate consistent work. The challenge is going where the work takes you. Touring is hard, and it takes a toll on relationships. Dave has found a balance in his life.

These days most jobs are within driving distance. I live in Minnesota, so I travel a lot to Iowa, North Dakota, South Dakota, Minnesota, and Wisconsin. I spent a month in Chicago earlier this year. It's not glamorous travel. But if you talked to my wife, she'd say I'm gone quite a bit because I'm away during the summer instead of there with the kids.

The nice thing about working near home is great during the school year. I get to drive my kids to school and I'm here when they get home. The life of a yoyo pro means if you have a show during the day, oftentimes it's only an hour long. Half an hour drive to get there, do the show, half hour drive home. You're only gone a couple of hours out of a whole day.

The gigs Dave had the most fun at were weddings. My family is Catholic and does the traditional wedding format of holding a ceremony at a church, then leaving the family hanging for hours and hours while the wedding party goes off and takes photos or maybe builds a house (it always feels that long). The wedding party arrives at a hall for the dinner, speeches by drunken relatives, then dancing. Dazzling Dave is the answer to that eternal lull in the middle.

Oftentimes here in the United States the wedding happens at a church. Then the guests go to a reception while the bridal party doesn't go straight to the reception. They either go bar hopping or get their pictures or whatever might be happening. All the guests stand around looking for something to do. So that's where I come in, it works out great to entertain those groups.

I asked Dave his most important piece of advice for an aspiring performer. He shares a little of his wisdom:

I always Walk the Dog because, as a true professional performer, you've got to be able to show the tricks that people know and love. You have to connect to the audience, so I take my metal yoyo and walk along the concrete because that kid wants to see.

Always "Walk the Dog." It's not about your yoyo, or the trick. It's about connecting with someone in something joyful, even for a moment.

Chih-Minh Tuan

A few years ago, I had the pleasure of meeting Chih-Minh Tuan. He sent a message to the Vancouver Yoyo Club group on Facebook looking to connect with some yoyoers. Why was he in town, you might ask? He's a performer in Cirque Du Soleil's "Kurios" show. That's right—there is a yoyoer in a major touring circus going all over the world!

Chih-Minh has competed multiple times at the World Yoyo Contest in the AP (Art and Performance) division. He delivered amazing acts, including one that landed him second place in 2013.

Cirque Du Soleil is based out of Quebec, Canada and is the largest circus production in the world. They run over a dozen shows around the world every year. Each show has a theme and a story where a character leads the audience through a fantastical world. "Kurios" is a glimpse inside the workshop of an inventor, full of steampunk imagery.

The character Chih-Minh Tuan plays was created for 2001 World Yoyo Champion Tomonari Ishiguro, (aka "Black"). When Black left the show, Cirque Du Soleil contacted Chih-Minh and asked him to join the show! Chih-Minh recreated the performance to suit his own style, which fit right in with the rest of the show's theme.

So, how does one earn a position in one of the largest theatrical production companies in the world? Chih-Minh gives the obvious answer:

"I started my career as a yoyo performer 15 years ago."

That's right—time and experience. Chih-Minh started in a similar position to Dazzling Dave, never sure when the next gig would appear. He performed at corporate parties and even on television.

After I finished college, I became a street performer. That's how I made my living until I joined Cirque Du Soleil. I went on 'China's Got Talent,' then competed at the World Yoyo Contest. I became kind of famous in Asia.

I've been on the World Yoyo Contest stage. It's incredibly stressful. I'm sure it pales in comparison to being on a national TV talent show! But those experiences prepared him to take up the call to join the circus.

I guess they chose me because I could really work with the music.

I can attest to that. My wife and I got tickets to see the show, and it was two hours of mind-boggling talent. After the show, we stuck around, and Chih-Minh gave us a backstage tour. It turns out that the performers have multiple jobs. His performance was as the Master of Time. He delivers perfectly choreographed yoyo tricks to music. Unlike competitors, his tricks are difficult enough to amaze, but simple enough to follow. When he wasn't on stage, he had other tasks, like driving a giant hand prop with four contortionists performing on top.

Traveling with a show is not as fun as people think. We travel the world, but it's more like travel between hotel and tent. We don't have enough time to travel in cities deeply. We perform nine shows per week, one day off per week. It's very hard work, and it takes a lot of time each day.

One of Chih-Minh's tasks each day is to manage his own costume and makeup. A staff runs the laundry (the circus has its own bank of industrial laundry machines) and a costumes repair workshop travels with the show. Most of the time when he's not on set Chih-Minh still needs to be nearby, so his social time is very limited. It seems like a hard way to live, but an exciting one!

I asked him his advice for aspiring performers looking to run off and join the circus. He says:

Make sure you love it, and you can handle doing things repeatedly. You will need to make your act stabilized but fluid. Find the balance between what an audience needs to see and what you enjoy doing. It's not about how difficult the trick is, it's about creating a performance that can hold the audience's attention.

Harrison Lee

Harrison Lee is a well known yoyoer and a local superstar in Vancouver. I live in the same city, so people spot me yoyoing in public and ask, "Hey do you know that yoyo kid?" Harrison busks, performs on stage, and does demonstrations for charity on a regular basis.

He got his start young and benefited from supportive parents. He discovered that the novelty and nostalgia of yoyo tricks opened doors and created opportunities—everything from busking at the local night market to yoyoing on stage with the band The Barenaked Ladies or a small part in a Seth Rogen film!

Was it a career path? Or would he have been better off working a regular teenager job? Harrison shares his thoughts:

> After competing for a couple of years, I started doing local performances in Vancouver at talent shows, events, and festivals. Yoyoing is a part-time job alongside my academics. I manage my yoyo performer business. I am student by day and yoyo performer by night. It has taught me the skills needed to be an entrepreneur.

> My income from being a yoyo performer will not replace a regular job. It's more about an opportunity to be an artist, and to showcase something different."

> Like Dazzling Dave, Harrison had to track down work in the beginning. Before long, work was finding him.

> "I have performed at most of the major festivals in the Lower Mainland. I have worked a variety of interesting private events. Everything from kid's birthday parties to corporate special events (Christmas parties and business conferences).

> I reached out to event organizers to see if they wanted a kid yoyo competitor. Over time I solidified myself as a legitimate performer. Word-of-mouth referrals and re-hires from organizers of past events became the norm.

Harrison received an invitation to speak at a TEDx Kids event. I got to share some of his excitement when they invited me to run a yoyo demo-table during intermission.

> *I have done quite a few TED related events. TEDx Kids Vancouver, TEDxSFU, and NinjaTED (the performing arts component of TedTalks). I was selected for these events through word-of-mouth referrals and previous performances. I did a lot of preparation for my talks. I had to plan my message, coordinate with the event organizers, and prepare yoyo routines to accompany my message. I was, of course, super nervous to perform. But I was also very proud to share my yoyo and art beyond our immediate community. It was great to have yoyo be appreciated by a broader audience.*

Harrison is a polished and engaging speaker. Like any skill, being in front of an audience or camera takes practice, and Harrison has had plenty! He continues to be a force in the Canadian yoyo scene and a busy performer.

Performance art is difficult. As we've seen, it takes more than competition-ready tricks. A yoyoer like me spends most of their time alone, crafting or learning tricks. I'm not worrying about what people will enjoy seeing when I finally post it on YouTube—at least, not beyond the few dozen who want to learn my tricks. I create for the sake of creating.

A performer creates an act, and then moulds it anew for each audience. The audience IS the show. They are the reason you are there. John Higby relies on props and big tricks to yoyo his way to success. Mark Hayward works with clever tricks and storytelling. Dazzling Dave Schultz plays to every audience with the simplest tricks and a big smile. Chih-Minh weaves a tale with music and movement. What they all have in common is the audience and the joy of this age-old toy.

Chapter 10: The Yoyopreneur

Entrepreneurs are a unique bunch. We enjoy stepping out on the ledge to have a peek over the side. You never know if there's someone down there you can sell a rope to! More likely we spend our time looking around for problems to solve. The person who invented the skateboard wanted to surf when the weather was bad. The person who invented rollerblades likely wanted to practice ice skating where no rink was available. Entrepreneurs are folks who ask questions and then make the answers into reality.

There are three main avenues for those with the entrepreneur spirit:

1. *Create an original design or work of art.*

2. *Modify or re-purpose an existing product.*

3. *Find a unique product and then find the right person to buy it.*

How to go about setting up a business as an entrepreneur is a topic for another book. Yet it's important to recognize the "Yoyopreneurs" who help the hobby grow—the folks who find their place in the yoyo world as the creators or middlemen providing yoyos to the rest of us.

The yoyo world is full of artists. Few of us figure out how to turn that skill into a business. The people in this next section are Yoyopreneurs—people who looked at some aspect of yoyo and thought, "I could do that better" or, "Why is no one doing this yet?"

The Maker and Modder

In the first decade of the 21st century, yoyo designers struggled to figure out what worked best. The result was that people bought yoyos and then made changes or modifications to increase performance or meet personal preferences. "Modding" became a common practice and led to many of the most common standard features we see on modern yo-yos today.

Changing the response system was the most common Mod. Starburst response (raised bumps that grab the string) and raised stickers made from a variety of materials were the standards of the day but led to inconsistent performance poor spin times. Modders would mount the yo-yo to a drill or a lathe and cut a groove near the bearing seat (after shaving off the starburst, if necessary) which they would then fill with silicone. This allowed the string less contact with the response material and increased spin times dramatically. Other changes to the response could include widening the gap of the yo-yo through the use of shims on the axle or doubling up on bearings - a mod known as "beefcaking".

Advanced modders could change the shape and the weight of a yoyo using a machine lathe. Changing the shape or adding weight rings to the rim could have a huge effect on weight distribution and change the feel of yo-yo overall. Master modders could change the shape and dynamics of a yo-yo so much as to render it unrecognizable, compared to the original, in shape and playability.

Very few modern yo-yos require any kind of modding to become playable today. They're ready to go out of the box. A player may choose to swap out the bearing for preference or change the response pads to flowable silicone, but none of those changes are required to make the yo-yos capable of advanced trick play.

Team Dollar Yoyo

About five years ago, a phenomenon hit the Facebook group "Yoyo BST & Talk"—the Dollar Tree yoyo. Most dollar store yoyos are complete garbage. For a brief time however, the Dollar Tree chain sold a metal yoyo with a ball bearing. It was...well, it was still garbage, but a better class of garbage. When they first appeared, people would offer them as a joke in trade for $100 plus yoyos. Yet some people started experimenting with mods, and it got ridiculous, so I made a separate group: Team Dollar Tree Yoyo.

A little patience and a few household supplies turned these dollar yoyos into something trick-worthy. Shave down the pads, clean the bearing, and you had an unresponsive yoyo! People hunted the stores, walking out with bags of yoyos. Someone figured out you could buy them from stores by the box—so I did. I must have gone through hundreds of them, modding them, reselling them, or just giving them away to kids. I put together a couple compilation videos of people playing with their modded "DTYY's." We even got t-shirts made! The fad didn't last long, as the chain sold out and then didn't restock, but it was fun while it lasted!

It was a little burst of ridiculous fun, the kind that comes around every few years in our community. The best part was the timing. This happened in the fall, and many people bought up the DTYY's they could find then donated them to Christmas toy drives. One delightful pair put together a short video in the style of the TV series Breaking Bad. They bought bags of the yoyos, bearing cleaner, and spray paint and filmed themselves cooking up some yoyos to give to charity! You can find this on YouTube by searching "Team Dollar Tree Yoyo Breaking Bad Tribute"

Modding for performance

Players who compete in the 2a division of contests (two-handed looping tricks) still need to mod their yoyos. It's a style that is highly personalized. Unlike other divisions, 2a players use inexpensive plastic yoyos. I've been told that the serious ones buy their yoyos by the box because they have to be modded right but only last a couple weeks of hard play! **Sammy Park** is a competitive 2a player who is a bit of a minimalist when it comes to modding his 2a throws. He explains:

> If the yoyo has a fixed gap, then I clean the bearing, lube it, and find the right pair of spacers for it. For plastic spacers, I usually just use them or sometimes sand them down. However, for metal spacers I try to mix and match sets, as some of them have different widths (such as loop 720, but for c3 initiators the spacers were a bit inconsistent which became a part of the modding). Then, for gap adjustable yoyos, I spend a lot of time trying to find the right gap. Then I try different lubricants and lubing methods for best feeling of play. (Some methods of lubing are mixing multiple variations, lubing the axle and not the bearing, changing the amount of lube, and lining the starburst). The process can take anywhere between 30 to 60 minutes per pair, including finding the optimal string length.

> When I get a new yoyo, the most I do is change the bearing for my preferred type and throw on a new string!

This brings us to those who used to take modding to the extreme. For them, the World Yoyo Contest used to host a special event: The Mod Contest. These players take a stock yoyo and turn it into something magical. They even start from scratch and craft their own yoyos for the purpose of doing something unique or so extreme that most manufactures wouldn't dare to try it. **Mr. Bist** was one of the more well-known of these modders.

Mr. Bist – Master Modder

> There are two kinds of yoyos I made: the ones I loved, and the ones loved by others. They rarely match. To me, an excellent yoyo must play awesome. But with modding, yoyoers like the crazy

stuff like lights and sounds. I think that's the reason MP3 and the Speaker yoyo had so much success. But they are heavy, slow, and definitely not good players.

I made the MP3 after Ben from YoyoFactory announced the whistling yoyo, saying 'This is art and innovation.' That was so funny to me, so, I machined the MP3 the day after I made the video. So funny! My graphic manager, Buttermouse inspired the Speaker. He made a very cool drawing of a yoyo with a speaker inside. When I saw it, I thought, 'Why not?' The style was very challenging to design. The magnet, put only in one cup, unbalanced the yoyo. I like this kind, but I consider it a clown—yoyo, just for fun. More or less, I like all the yoyos I made, but the technical ones, to me, are the best.

It's interesting to hear Mr. Bist talk about the difference between his yoyos—the ones designed to be great players vs. the off-the-wall crazy designs. I think my favourite of his was the "Ice Yoyo." He created a mould and made a yoyo out of ice—and it worked!

The yoyo world is full of artists. They look at a yoyo and think, "Something is missing." Some artists work with paint and decorate yoyos by hand, creating one of a kind works of art. Others scale up and use dye or the anodizing process to create batches of eye-catching designs. I dabbled in airbrush painting for a while.

I stopped when I realized I'd need to invest in better equipment and a dedicated painting space to keep going, but I had fun creating art and still have a couple of these yoyos in my collection. Below are some stories of yoyo artists who continued where I left off, and mastered the finished product.

Brett Grimes – Airbrush Master

Brett Grimes started painting yoyos before multi-color anodized yoyos became the standard. People experimented with powder coating, complex laser engraving, and paint. Brett says:

The painting thing has always been in my blood, I have been painting since I was a teenager. I am 46 now and continue to be a person who likes to tinker. One day we were talking about a white yoyo and how cool it would look on film. White is not a color you can anodize. One day the lightbulb went off in my head, and I painted a One Drop Yoyos M1. It was an instant hit online, so I started doing some other things, and again it snowballed from there. Within a few weeks I had people asking me to paint theirs. I liked the idea that someone had a one-off custom yoyo that might be collectible at some point.

I was doing what I called rainbow splash, a multi-colored finish. It wasn't long before someone figured out how to do it with anodizing. I then began working with swirled paint, which is hydro dipping the yoyo into a thin film of paint suspended on water. [When] someone else figured out how do to the same with anodizing, the bottom fell out for my art. I let it fizzle out naturally.

The biggest challenges with paint and powder-coated finishes were balance and durability. Yoyos are fiddly things. If the weight isn't balanced right, they become hard to play with. Powder coating and painting both added layers of material, and the weight was very challenging to keep even. Anodizing, in comparison, adds fractions of a millimetre of material, and is a far more durable finish.

Anodizing is a complex process. It requires patience, precision, and care. The process involves soaking your aluminum in an electrified acid bath. I'm not going to try to explain the science, but the result is a hardened layer of material on the surface. It has the added bonus of allowing aluminum to absorb dye. This process is superior to paint, as the color becomes part of the aluminum and can't chip off.

The market has moved on, but anyone out there with a Brett Grimes painted yoyo has a beautiful little piece of yoyo history!

Ray Smith – Anodizer Extraordinaire

Ray Smith is one of my fellow Canadian yoyo makers. He got into the business around the same time I started yoyoing (2009). He started yoyoing because his kid caught the yoyo bug. Like many, Ray kept going long after his kid lost interest. Where Ray differed from most yoyoers was in making the fateful observation:

*"You know, how hard could it be to make a yoyo?
It's just a yoyo!"*

The answer is—that it's much harder than you think. Ray created his brand, MonkeyfingeR Design (MFD), and began learning. While learning to design a yoyo, he discovered that yoyo anodizing was an underdeveloped industry. A housepainter by day, Ray took up anodizing at night. He dove into this new creative outlet, finding artistic fulfillment that he didn't get from painting the walls of a house.

The common practice at the time was to use a single color for your aluminum, with at most one other color splattered on. Ray skipped straight to figuring out the hardest color options. To this day, MonkeyfingeR Design is synonymous with the most creative yoyo anodizing on the planet.

Anodizing is a complicated process. A few years ago I stayed with Ray for a few days after the Canadian National Yoyo Championship. Just for fun he walked me through the basics of anodizing. I'd been dabbling in airbrush painting yoyos and was curious about anodizing. We went into his garage and five hours later we had two yoyos custom anodized. The process is time consuming and involves layers of work and many careful steps.

I asked Ray a few questions, starting with the big one: Why anodizing as an art form?

There is always something else in my life. This just seems to be the latest of what I'm working on. Before yoyos I was making furniture, playing the drums, sketching, and painting. This was the next evolution of the creative process in my life. The challenge is always the learning curve. But that's the part I enjoy! It's great when you get to the ending and you figure it out, but the fun lies in the journey.

When we came on the scene there were a few outliers creating some funky cool stuff but not in the mainstream. We started out right to the deep end of the pool with a four-color splash which I had never seen before. To tell you the truth the first colorway ("Mizaru") didn't do great. People thought it was too busy. There were only a few who bought that very first run.

Over the next few years we figured out how to apply complex techniques that looked simple. You'll find in our designs now that there are multiple colors but simple in the layout. Where you see a solid color, there is usually something going on within the splash. Chances are there is a three-tone acid wash behind the splash to make it pop. The trick is finding ways to keep the complex visuals from being overwhelming.

Ten years later, other shops have learned similar techniques and extended them. Four colors on a yoyo is no longer an unusual sight. So, what keeps MFD innovating? Why push on?

When I started, we were doing the only complex stuff out there. Slowly, the other anodizers caught up to speed and now create complicated stuff. It's not the complexity that I enjoy the most, it's the cleverness of different colors and how they put them together that catches my eye. I don't think I've seen the end of the road of the creation process for the color layouts. There's always something left to discover.

I know that there are some companies that will do printing techniques and complex designs. I feel the nicest stuff lies in the abstract freehand layout where things are not the same for each yoyo.

I would say the best place to start is where I started. I went to a store called Caswell and bought an anodizing kit. I don't recommend piecing it together because you will end up spending more money. Spend the $1,500 for a small bucket system and believe it or not at two and four parts at a time you can do everything that I do. You just need to figure it out.

The true art lies in the consistency. It's easy to pull off one color on one part at a time. It's much more difficult to pull off 20 yoyos that are the same color, layout, and brightness. That's where the real art lies. The other advice is cleaning. Surgically clean everything. Once you start the process, you never touch

*the part again until you're finished. Remember that and
[you] will have good results.*

Despite complex anodizing becoming the norm, Ray is still
very successful. Every yoyo he releases sells out in short order.
The fact that he does the anodizing himself also allows him to
create short run special editions, which is not a viable option for
most brands. When I make yoyos, the shop wants me to do 50
pieces per color!

I suspect that Ray will continue to come up with clever
techniques that keep him ahead of the curve. If you are curious
about anodizing, go for it! Just get the right safety equipment
(goggles and respirator) and learn as much as you can before
you start!

One material that makes for good yoyos is Delrin (POM). It's
a dense plastic that can be machined like aluminum. In the last
few years, a handful of modern modders discovered that it's
really easy to dye! Delrin yoyos come in half a dozen solid colors.
I love this innovation, as it allows me as a manufacturer to offer
more variety to customers.

Jeff Anderson – Dye Master

I met Jeff Anderson through Facebook, as with so many of my
yoyo world friends. If I recall correctly, he was looking for Delrin
yoyos to experiment on. In 2018, I released a yoyo called "The
Sk8r" made out of Delrin. One downside to using this type of
plastic is that it's expensive and is available in a limited range of
colors—at least until some industrious yoyoers figured out you
could use fabric dye to create the most amazing patterns and
designs on your yoyo.

I asked Jeff to share his yoyo story and how he ended up
as a yoyo artist.

*A few contests later I met a guy who was showing off
dyed yoyos (hi Stephen). I always loved the thought of
modding yoyos. Back in my day, we had to mod them to*

make them any good. I had always thought the old school dyes of John Higby and Eric Wolff were so awesome. Stephen talked to me about dyeing out in front of the venue [and] gave me some pointers when I said I always wanted to try it.

Later on I tried it on the only Delrin yoyo I had. It was a failure. I had no idea what I was doing. So I set out to learn more... reading about dyes and how the plastic is affected by it, talking with other yoyo dyers about time and temperature, how masking works, how colors blend... I wanted to learn as much as I could.

I taught myself how to do different things with dye, experimenting on used yoyos I bought for cheap in the Facebook group. I enjoyed doing it, and the community seemed to enjoy the final products. I dyed over 50 yoyos in that time and probably a dozen counterweights. People noticed and began asking for commissions. They'd tag me in listings for yoyos that could be dyed and asked me for pointers. It made me feel like a real part of the community. This summer companies started talking with me about dyeing yoyos for them and last month I ended up dyeing 151 of other people's yoyos. Wow!

Now I've found a place in the community, and it really helps give me a sense of family and of personal identity.

Jeff is a great guy, and it's been a pleasure to get to know him. His dye work has become a regular feature on Rain City Skills yoyos!

String Makers

Yoyo string is a funny product. It's critical to the hobby. Without string, a yoyo is a fancy paperweight. As I shared earlier, I discovered the online yoyo world because my students ran out of yoyo string and I needed to find more. You can't just take any old piece of string and tie it onto your yoyo. Well, you can, but I wouldn't recommend it.

Before the 1900s, that's exactly what people did, but a regular old string tied to the axle limited you to basic tricks. "The Sleeper," the fundamental trick of all modern yoyoing, was impossible. This all changed with the innovation of a string that folded in on itself and twisted, creating a loop for the yoyo axle to sit in. The result was a yoyo that could spin within that loop!

You need more than run of the mill string to play with a yoyo. In essence, to create a yoyo string, you begin by twisting about two metres (seven feet) of individual threads together. You then fold this in half and twist it the other way. If you maintain the right tension, you'll have a string that will sit slack without looking like a plate of spaghetti. If you can find a consistent system for crafting your string, you're ready to move on to the issue of player preference.

Yoyoers like their string to be predictable. They have preferences and want consistency. Some players change strings a couple of times a day. Others use the same string on their yoyo for weeks or months. I knew one guy who used the same string until it broke and would pick up string that other club members discarded. He wasn't short of cash; he just liked the way a well worn-in string played. He didn't understand people wasting money throwing away perfectly good string. I'm the opposite; I change my string daily. I like the feeling of "bounce" you get in a brand-new string.

The big question most players have to ask themselves is: bulk or boutique? Many players are fine with the least expensive yoyo string they can get. I remember early in my yoyo career one of the kids in the club bought a 1000 pack of string. He wore it around his neck like a scarf the day he brought it to show off. Others swear by a specific brand of hand-crafted string, purchased in 5 or 10 packs for up to $2 per string! I did that early in my yoyo career; I spent way too much money on strings from Canadian string maker YoyoGstrings. At this point, I just use the bulk string I order for Rain City Yoyos, but a well-crafted boutique string is easy to appreciate.

So, what makes one string "better" than another? There are variations of thickness, thread count, and thread quality. Each maker uses a slightly different setup, with variations in tension, twist, and color. Some makers, like Daniel Kessler at 24K Whips, use a time-consuming technique to create visually stunning string. His string plays great, and if you are someone who collects yoyos for display, it's a must-have. **Jeremy Park** of Zipline Strings focuses on high-quality materials and precision-crafted string.

Jeremy Park – Zipline Strings

Jeremy Park runs his business out of his home, with a hand-crafted string twisting rig. Rich colors, consistent tension, and carefully tailored thread combinations are the result. Every brand of thread is different, and every color works a little differently. White thread is thinner than red, and sometimes coarser. String making is a time-consuming task. I asked Jeremy to share why he took it on.

There's something personal and special about a handmade product. You can feel the love and passion behind it. My journey began with my obsession with yoyos and yoyo strings. I purchased so many different brands of polyester strings over the years. While they all did their job, I never settled on anything being 'the one,' I kept searching for something new.

I recall conversations in my head as I would try out new strings. 'I wish these were firmer' or 'Hmmmm... these might be better if they could cut air a little faster.' 'What if these were more consistent from string to string' and 'I wish these didn't go limp so quickly' etc.

The way I make strings is a by-product of countless hours and long nights perfecting my recipe. I sought the perfect polyester and/or hybrid material yoyo string. I also wanted this to be a family project. Doing something I'm passionate about with the people I love is one of the most enjoyable and rewarding ways I can think of to spend my time!

After much research and experimentation, and after many failed trial runs, I reached one of those 'Eureka!' moments which stopped me dead in my tracks. I realized that I could pull off a couple of bind tricks that were difficult to do with the yoyo I used for testing. Shortly after this discovery, I tried the same binds again, and again, flawlessly, and before I knew it, I got chills up my spine, 'THIS IS THE ONE!!!' After additional trials and tweaks I had my formula. It became the basis for how all the ZipLine Strings are now made.

I come up with the formulas, spin the strings, and do lots of testing. My wife, Danielle, helps with the final stages of this process. The finishing touches, including searching for quality issues. Our two daughters, Kaylee and Adysen, work together *to button up our product. The snipping, tying, writing cards, packaging, and shipping.*

Our intention isn't to compete with bulk string manufacturers, and we do not have plans to sell in bulk. Our small business can only produce limited quantities. Our goal is to make a premium quality yoyo string that feels familiar, yet different enough to feel special. It has to excel during extended performance. Furthermore, if we can produce a five pack of strings that will hang tough with a 10 pack of string, we'll take that as a win!

This is a product made with our own hands, using high quality materials with a great deal of love and attention. We plan to always make it a point to offer something more than just the strings themselves by making each order special—giving each a personal touch. This extra effort makes all the difference.

Coming up with a recipe and a technique is a whole different thing than running a business. You need branding, advertising, and you need to build a strong reputation. Zipline has a good recipe for that as well.

When I felt that I had something special, and I knew that I could recreate it consistently, I decided that I was finally ready to have other people try it out. I sent some off to a few yoyo players who also reviewed yoyo products. I figured that they must have experience with different yoyo strings. They could offer me honest feedback I could use to making a better product. At the very least, I'd be able to know if I was into something or if I'd only made a string that was special to me.

Tom Velto was the first real fan of the product. He seemed to genuinely love it—to where he described it as the best string ever made! Other reviewers agreed; I had a hit!

At the time I had one string blend (Slushy Edition) and three colors, and I was making them one string at a time. I later worked with a friend of mine to engineer a string rig capable of spinning up to five strings at a time. It also had the benefit of greater accuracy and consistency than with my one-off method.

I started selling privately in very small quantities. I took orders though email or private message on our social media accounts. It didn't take long for me to start a waiting list. It grew to where it became too stressful to manage, so we stopped selling for a while. We built a website, a webstore, and produced enough product to stock our store with legit quantities and varieties.

We officially opened the online store on June 1st, 2017 and by the following morning nearly everything sold out. I stayed up all night assembling and packing orders (this is before we had a good system for shipping). When Danielle came to see what I was up to at 10:30 am, she asked 'Did you even come to bed last night?' My reply? 'No, I've been right here, packing orders all night... I think we might be in the string making business!' I let out a half-asleep chuckle.

My next question was the big one: Are you making any money? A business turns a profit—a hobby not so much.

This endeavor is by no means a 'big money maker.' It's a passion project, for sure. I still work a full-time day job and my wife is a full-time mom who assists me with the string business in her spare time. My single income isn't quite enough to cover all our monthly expenses. So I've been running some sort of side business ever since my first daughter, Kaylee, was born 11 years ago.

That being said, we do have to treat this business as a legit form of income. We take very little from the string business— just enough to supplement our monthly household expenses. The rest gets reinvested back into the business and/or used to cover operational costs. Raw materials, sponsorship residuals, merchandise, capital reserves... the list goes on!

That's not bad. A hobby that pays for itself, brings the family together, and provides a little extra income. I'd say that's a success! Finally, the big question: Why Zipline over anyone else? Many competitive players go through handfuls of string during a practice session. They aren't Jeremy's target market.

Above anything else, we aim to project love in everything that we do. And we strive to make our products enhance your boutique yoyo experience. When you open a package from ZipLine, we want it to feel special and that it was handled with care—for you personally. We produce them in small batches and spun with more focus, so the quality control is high. We examine each string, and each string passes through our hands to feel for kinks or anomalies. Often, the strings get looked over and felt two or three times from first spin to packaging.

A lot of passion went into the creation of each blend we make, but we don't want it to stop there. Each blend has its own artwork, and each colorway has a unique name. We run string naming contests and/or polls, so the community feels involved.

Customer care is very important to us—both my wife and I come from careers with a strong focus in customer service. How we interact with our customers is much like how we interact with a long-time friend. We get to know them, and we care about them.

In application, let's say you buy a boutique yoyo for $85 and you're about to unpackage and throw it for the first time. There's something extra special about lacing it up with a boutique *string for that 'first throw' experience. Premium string is an extension of the premium yoyo you invested your hard-earned dollars in. The whole experience feels more complete, more special, and more premium. At least try it for the first throw— there's nothing like it. Sure, slap on your bulk string every time after, but for that first throw, make it special.*

I love his explanation. When I released my first yoyo, the "Hipster Highlife," I was going for that high-end collectible feel. There was no question in my mind that I'd use a handmade, custom-blended string to match each colour of yoyo. I wanted customers to get that special feeling.

Your average player will use up that string then go back to their regular string. But for the collector, that yoyo will sit on display. It's up to you to decide if you want that display piece to have a generic bulk string attached, or something a little more.

Daniel Kessler – 24K Whips

I collaborated with Daniel in 2018-2019 to release a yoyo using his string brand. We called it "The Retrorocket." Daniel blended together colors of thread to match the color of the yoyos. He uses an exclusive technique to create strings that change color mid-string. His strings straddle the line between function and art.

I picked up yoyoing as a hobby a few years ago when I found a Yomega Brain yoyo at a Walmart. I started researching the hobby and discovered that yoyoing evolved since I was in the third grade. Had me hooked from the start. I found myself yoyoing everywhere I went, grocery stores, work, school, everywhere.

Eventually I ran into a 'pay-wall' that some people can't advance through. Start buying supplies to maintain this newfound habit, or make my own. And so this began my string making journey.

String making is crucial. Anyone can go to their favorite store or website and buy generic machine-made yoyo string. But I was on a mission to make custom strings designed for each player's use. It took almost a year before I perfected my formula for the perfect string. I combined luxury and performance into a solid line of communication between you and your yoyo.

Since then, I've learned that strings are more important than anyone can imagine. A yoyo journey starts at the end of a string. And believe me the tension is intense! Always progressing and keeping up with this modern world of return tops. I have catered to some of the community's biggest names and collaborated with some of its greatest minds.

I chose yoyo string as my business of choice because it's the one thing you'll always need. No string? Your yoyo is a fancy paperweight.

From fixed axle to 5a, I've made enough strings to give the world its playtime. But the business isn't easy. It takes a huge amount of patience and even more time. For example, a standard single colored yoyo string can take two or three minutes to make. But one of our specialty 24k Whips Fades takes patience to make. I have to loom each individual strand to the next to create the most delectable colors that flawlessly change mid string! Phenomenal indeed!

But colors aren't everything. What makes a great string is the attention to details. The tension preserved, the length, the strength of material, type of material. It ALL matters. Changing even a single thread can change an entire string's make up— art!

What I like best is how much fun Daniel is having making strings for people. He's not trying to compete with the big bulk brands; his goal is to create the perfect tool for the individual. His strings speak luxury, and that's something that has its place in any hobby.

The Retail Store

A few years ago, I got the bright idea to set up an online retail store and sell yoyos. I was very active in the Canadian yoyo community. The Vancouver Yoyo Club was very active, and I was supplying a lot of their yoyos, since it's hard to get good yoyos in Canada. Shipping is expensive, and we pay extra import taxes. I figured there was enough of a market to support a small online store. So, Return Top Shop was born. It was a heck of a ride for the two years I ran it.

I learned a few things. For one, there actually weren't enough Canadian customers to keep the store afloat, so I had to carve a place out in the American market. This meant competition and smaller profit margins—especially after I paid shipping and import taxes. The biggest challenge was time. Getting orders to the post office two or three times per week while also working a full-time job became tedious. I ended up using a courier, which in turn increased my costs.

I started Return Top Shop around the same time that Mrs. Yoyothrower and I moved in with her father to take care of him. My late mother-in-law had been an avid collector. The basement in the house was full of everything from Barbies (a 2nd edition in-box!), to sports collectables, to a room with at least a thousand teddy bears. As we cleaned it out, we turned up boxes and boxes of small toys, trinkets, and trading cards that had little to no value. So, as an advertising gimmick, I included a handful of "extras" with each order yoyo I filled. This became a marketing hit. People would receive their order from me, then immediately post a picture of all their loot!

Return Top Shop was a marvellous learning experience, and while I didn't make money running the store, at least I didn't lose any! The day came when I realized I didn't want to sell other people's yoyos; I wanted more creative control. So, I closed the doors on Return Top Shop and put my time and money behind my fledgling brand, Rain City Skills. For all its ups and downs, the experience of running the online store set me up for success in this new endeavor.

While I didn't find success selling other people's goods, there are a handful of yoyoers who make it work. Steve Reeder went one step further than I did—he runs a real, brick-and-mortar toy store. That means he does everything I did, plus managing employees and juggling the costs of keeping up a physical location. He added yoyos to his store for much the same reason I started Return Top Shop— to bring the joy of yoyos to his country (in this case, Austria). My hat is off to anyone who manages to make a retail store work in the era of Amazon and Walmart! Steve shares some of his story below:

Steve Reeder (Stevie Ray Kwon)

We opened the Motmot Shop in 2006, as more of a creative workspace than a proper retail shop. Over time our shop became more of a proper retail space. We sell our T-shirt designs and we've carried many secondary items over the years. Art and design books, zines, paper crafts, etc.... However, none of the other items we've sold ever really clicked and caught on the way we would have liked.

My history with yoyos goes back to about 1987, when I was in my first year of high school. There was a bit of a yoyo craze at my school. I remember having a Green Duncan Imperial, and later getting a BC Rainbow, which was great until the axle broke. Those were great, and I learned the basic tricks for the time—looping, Around the World, Rock the Cradle, etc.

Fast forward to the 90s and I stumbled into a hobby shop in Fullerton, California. I saw some amazing new yoyos with tiny bearings for axles, so I bought one, a Spintastics Glow Tornado. It's still in my collection. I remember carrying it around and throwing it often in college. I even tried to impress a girl in school. Her reaction was something like, 'Will you put that thing away?'

A few decades later and I lived in another country, Austria. My partner and I opened up a fun little T-shirt and gift shop, and somehow, we manage to have a family of our own. One day my oldest daughter asked if she could use my yoyos, and I happily obliged her. This sent me down the Google rabbit hole and I kept hearing about something called an unresponsive yoyo. Of course I needed one of these...immediately. The question 'Where can I find an unresponsive yoyo in Vienna?' came back with a resounding 'You can't!'

It became an obsession. I ordered a hybrid yoyo, a Basecamp Sherpa, because I was too chicken to go fully unresponsive. The yoyo arrived and after a few attempts I got the yoyo to bind!

But there was still something nagging at me. There was no place to buy a yoyo in Vienna. I kept thinking it would be great if someone opened up a yoyo shop. 'Someone should do something about that!' The proverbial lightbulb went off in my head...'Hey, we have some shelf space, let's carry yoyos!'

So after a few e-mails, and a day trip to Prague, I sent off our first order. Within a few days our first shipment from Yoyo Factory arrived. I felt like a kid on Christmas morning! In what could only have been a good omen, within 10 minutes of opening the first box of yoyos, a young man named Niko peeped into our shop. He noticed the yoyos, and remarked that he was a thrower, and that it was cool that a local shop was carrying yoyos. Niko then performed a barrage of advanced yoyo tricks! 'Cool, I'll be back,' he said before disappearing. A good sign on the first day.

Having the yoyo shop in our city has made me deal with the business side of the yoyo world, warts and all. It's not that bad. The truth is, I really love to throw, so any added work is worth it. When I was a teenager I was heavily into freestyle skateboarding (skateboard tricks on flat ground). Yoyoing is the closest thing that gives me that same feeling of learning new manoeuvres. I love the feeling that learning a new trick or element brings. When someone asks me to do a trick, I am always happy to oblige them. The look on their faces when I do a gyroscopic flop or a fingerspin makes me feel like I'm 16 again.

So, far we haven't had any broken windows, but we've had a fair share of dinged yoyos. An unfortunate off-string yoyo flew out of our shop and onto the sidewalk and into the street one day.

I've seen some people balk at the price. I remember one neighbourhood kid calling his mom to ask if he could buy a yoyo. He told her the yoyo he wanted cost €23 (USD $25). I could hear the mom on the other end say something to the extent of 'What!? €23 for a yoyo? It's your money!' This was while he was talking on what was easily a €700 smartphone.

The local kids are a constant source of humor, the funniest was when a friend's 8-year-old son came in with his 'girlfriend.' When he started yoyoing she said, 'You better impress me!' And the boy got nervous and started to mess up his trick, Rock the Baby, and then he said, 'The yoyo's not working right!'

One customer that stood out was a woman who appeared to be in her mid 50s. She was really good at old-school tricks, Loop the Loop. You could tell that she had put some practice into it. I don't know why I was surprised, but I was.

I also have a day job as a graphic designer and illustrator, and I had the opportunity to take a class by a very well known and respected artist named Glenn Vilppu. Glenn is over 80 years old, but he still seems like a kid at heart in a lot of ways. During my two-day workshop with him, I busted out some yoyo tricks and everyone's collective jaw dropped. After the day's workshop, I opened up after hours and Glenn bought three Recess First Base yoyos. It turns out he actually had a pretty solid throw and catch, proving that you're never too old to start.

One very great chance encounter involved a bike messenger delivering something to our shop. After he dropped off our package, he noticed our yoyos and did some modern tricks. It turns out that he had been throwing for a while. When the last Austrian contest took place in 2016, he had lost contact with the yoyo scene. He also bought a new yoyo that day.

Vienna has a decent number of advanced yoyo players. I feel like I dodged a bullet in a way. Some cities or entire countries only have one or two throwers. I also feel that it's an interesting mix of people from very different backgrounds. Our core group consists of a pastor, a photographer, a chemist, an engineer, a technician, two social workers, a theologian, and some high school students. We've also been lucky to have visiting throwers from Argentina, Lithuania, Spain, Norway, and Israel.

I feel good about the fact that now there are hundreds of yoyos getting in the hands of people who wouldn't have tried it otherwise.

I think Steve undersells the value of a physical store in terms of building community. When I used to show up at the Vancouver Yoyo Club every single week, we had a huge community of skilled players. When life got too busy to attend as often, that dropped off. It's easy for folks to discover yoyo on the internet, but stumbling on a YouTube video will never be as inspiring as walking into a shop and learning from a real-live human.

Chapter 11: The Reviewer

When shopping for a new toy, gadget, book, etc., the first thing I generally do is read reviews. I want to know what other people, ideally with experience in the field, have to say. If I'm shopping online, viewing YouTube videos that show the product in action help me narrow down my choices.

With so many yoyos on the market, it's hard to make decisions about where to spend your money— particularly when you are looking at spending hundreds of dollars! The descriptions in retail stores are good, but are obviously biased in favor of sales. The specifications and pictures only tell you so much. Hearing another yoyoer, professional or otherwise, talk about a yoyo and show you how it plays is huge.

To have legitimacy as a reviewer, you need to be critical— pointing out faults as well as good points. Unfortunately, as with any other niche in society, you get tribalism. A review that criticizes a favorite brand can be met with vitriol. It's not common, but I've seen more than one person pushed away from doing quality reviews because of this. Another challenge is bias. People get to keep the products they review. That's a nice perk, but it can lead to more positive results, as reviewers are motivated to keep the company happy so they will send more. Luckily, yoyoers tend to be honorable. Below are five interviews with yoyoers who hold a place of trust and value in the yoyo review community.

Chris Allen and YoYoSkills

Chris Allen is a man of many hats. He has been a contest organizer, a yoyo teacher, and the person who set the standard for online yoyo reviews. For many years, yoyoskills.com was the go-to place for general yoyo news. Today, there are dozens of people reviewing yoyos. When Chris started out, there was a gap in the market that needed filling.

When I started yoyoskills.com in 2008-2009, there weren't many general yoyo websites. Extremespin.com and yoyonation.com had forums and there were websites for manufacturers. At the time I was dabbling in web design, graphic design, and project management. I was looking to cut my teeth on something new. I didn't have any kids yet, so I spent a lot of free time working on this idea for a website. I found a domain name registration site and, on a whim, tried yoyoskills.com. It was available and I jumped at it!

Then I had to decide what I wanted to do with it. Did I want to open a store? Did I want to open my own forum? There was another yoyo website called YoyoBox.com but it wasn't very active. I wrote an article for them, and it received a pretty good reception, but the site just wasn't very active. I decided to start over and build a yoyo centric website with a style like Gawker or Gizmodo. These niche blog sites only catered to one sort of topic. So, I decided to make one of those for yoyoing. I started writing articles and reviews. I posted links on the forums and because I wasn't connected to any store or manufacturer, and it took off!

I started out with a weekly review. I created a format and posted the articles with nice pictures and links to all the stores that had the yoyo in stock. After a while yoyoskills.com started getting attention. I noted that usually a week after I put up a review, stores would go from a couple dozen in stock to sold out. The stores and manufacturers noticed as well, and I started to receive products to review. It was cool to realize that my little website was having an impact on the success of yoyo sales.

I was at the point where I was getting a new yoyo on my doorstep practically every week from all over the world. I told all these manufacturers that if you send me your product, I'll review it, but it's not going to be a guaranteed favorable review. I'm going to put it through its paces.

There were plenty of yoyos that were just terrible. I didn't hold back in the in the product reviews. I also had my friends, who I knew would give me different opinions, to help as second testers. I wanted to make sure I wasn't an outlier.

Whenever a manufacturer asked for the product back, I always shipped out of my own pocket. But I never took down the reviews. It was a great partnership for everyone. The reviews got enough attention that I started writing articles, highlighting videos, and creating daily content. It kind of snowballed from there.

YoYoSkills became one of the biggest, most visited yoyo related website. The analytics I was getting showed that I was getting half a million clicks every day. I had to step back when my family expanded, and now YoYoSkills is part of the Skill Toy Network. I like to think that I helped the evolution of the yoyo community online.

Chris set the bar for yoyo reviews. I wrote a weekly guest spot for a short time after Chris spotted my blog. If I recall, his message to me was something like "You write well, and often. Want to write for Yoyoskills?" I only wrote a few articles before Chris's life took him in a different direction, but I guess that was my first real writing commission! No one since has created as many detailed and useful written reviews. Most reviewers these days have moved on technology-wise and do their reviews on YouTube. The visual format lets people get a better picture of what a yoyo is going to look like in their hands and feel like on the string. You can do that with photos, but it's not quite the same as watching someone unbox their new toy!

Thomas Velto – Throws n' Brews

Throws n' Brews is a YouTube channel run by Thomas Velto. Tom puts out a few videos each week, ranging from yoyo reviews to discussions of the politics of the sport. His method is rather different from Chris Allen's. Tom uses his cell phone camera to film an energetic and thoughtful review of a yoyo. He starts with the "unboxing" experience, shares his first impressions of the design, then puts a string on the yoyo and plays! He outlines the most common design features and compares the yoyo under review to other yoyos. Some of the topics he covers include the "Do's and Don'ts of Contest Travel," "Why are Yoyo's so Expensive?" and "Random Tuesday Thoughts."

In 2018, I shared a hotel room with Tom during the USA National Yoyo Contest. We took a few minutes one evening to do an interview, which was a lot of fun. He shares some thoughts about his journey to yoyo internet stardom:

> I got into yoyoing the way most guys my age did—the Yoyo Boom of the 90s. I asked my Mom and Dad for a Yomega Fireball. My mom had to get to Walmart at 5am the day they restocked to get one! I played with that thing until it broke. My dad said to me one day, 'You know that's cheating,' to which I responded, 'What are you talking about?' He told me that when he was a kid, yoyos were made out of wood and had a fixed axle (the Fireball had a more advanced 'transaxle'). I went out and got a Tom Kuhn wood yoyo and played with those for the next 20 years.

> When I got back into yoyoing, I wanted to build up my collection. But I noticed that there weren't many guys doing consistent and frequent yoyo reviews on YouTube. I figured I'd give it a shot. My first couple videos weren't very good, but they started catching on. The more I did and lots of people seemed to like them and find them helpful. I am a guitar player and there are a few guys on YouTube like Rob Chapman and Ryan Bruce who I go to for guitar gear information. I guess my inspiration was to be sort of like that, but for yoyo.

> Why do I do this? More than anything it's the interaction with the community. If I can help someone make the right decision when they pick out their next favorite yoyo, that's what I want to do.

Plus, it's fun for me! After a year, my YouTube channel is starting to generate some revenue. Nothing close to what I've put into it, but the goal is to have it paying for itself once I'm two years in. With any luck, paying for my hobbies as well!

I've got my fingers crossed for him. It's not easy making money off YouTube in a niche as small as yoyo, but if anyone can do it, it's someone with Thomas's big personality!

Dylan Kowalski

Dylan Kowalski is a mixed martial arts (MMA) fighter. He got into yoyo unboxing and reviews while taking some down time due to injuries and discovered a passion for sharing his thoughts on YouTube. Dylan has a unique personality that comes across as a no-nonsense honesty.

It happened by accident. I've had a YouTube channel since I graduated high school in 2005. I only used it a little and mostly for random home videos. In 2010, I kind of put yoyo on the back burner because I was so involved in MMA and trying to become a pro fighter. After my third fight, I tore my ACL, so I started doing more yoyo again while I was hurt.

It had been a few years (five years?) and I wanted some new yoyos. I saw a bunch of "Magic Yoyos" and stuff that was super cheap. I looked for reviews and there weren't any. I got a couple cheap throws, and I reviewed them for others in my situation. When I started checking other people's evaluations, I noticed there was a void in the market. In all these reviews, the people weren't using the yoyo, just holding it and talking. I also noticed they seemed very serious and kind of boring. So, I tried [to] make them funny and be myself. I try to do all my videos in one take, so it is true and organic.

In late 2016, I completely tore both my lateral and medial meniscus, leaving me with no cartilage or ligaments in my right knee. This took my injury from a little problem to career ending. I started uploading videos way more because I had a lot of free time and was having surgery, etc.

I usually buy anything that is cheap or gets a lot of comments. Over three grand last year went to buying yoyos, so I try to make videos that will get views, otherwise I lose money.

I need about 10,000 views to pay for a $10 yoyo, so these are more profitable for me. The cheap yoyos get way more views than expensive ones. I accept anything people want to send me. I use Facebook and Instagram and Reddit, but YouTube is my main traffic source.

Dylan's videos are entertaining. He gives a great breakdown of the design features and performance, and isn't afraid to point out flaws. If the yoyo is terrible, he tosses it in the pool. The revenue from YouTube is an interesting point to consider. In my seven years doing tutorials, I've drawn in about $250 in ad revenue, averaging about 500 views per video. I was once interviewed by a Grade 6 student who wanted to know for a class project how one went about being a "Professional YouTuber." I think they were surprised to learn how much work went in, and how little money came back out. As Dylan mentioned, if you draw $1 for every 1000 views, you are doing well. Yoyoers on YouTube tend to be in it for the intrinsic reward of helping others and sharing what they know.

Yoyo Joe

Joe shares his process:

I love watching technology review videos. That's what got me into yoyo reviewing. I watch channels such as MKBHD, Unbox Therapy, and more. I like the high focus on the quality of their videos. In the beginning, I didn't have much; my mom's camcorder, a junky laptop, and a free editing software. Although I didn't have much, I focused on creating the best, highest quality reviews.

As time went on, I began getting some traction on my various social media platforms. People began to notice the effort I put into my videos (the editing, the video quality, the speaking), and it felt good. I earned recognition for my hard work, both satisfying and motivating. Before, I would just make reviews for the sake of making reviews. But now, I had something more. Something special. I had an audience.

I started out making reviews on yoyos I had purchased in the past. My goal was to guide future yoyo buyers to the right decision. I decided that my gear wouldn't cut it, and I began to do extra chores, mow lawns, monetize my videos. Over time, I gathered a substantial amount of money, which I invested back into my brand. I bought a professional DSLR camera, a computer, and some lighting and sound equipment. Things began to move quickly after that.

I'll never forget the first time I received a message from a company wanting to send me a yoyo for review. In the past, I received gratification for my work via YouTube comments, personal messages, interactions at yoyo contests. Now, I was actually receiving a product. This caught on like wildfire. After I received my first yoyo from a company for review, they kept coming (and still come!). Reviews are something I enjoy and I hope to continue making them. I absolutely love it when yoyoers come up to me at contests or message me talking about how they bought a specific yoyo they love because of my review. That's what keeps me motivated to keep creating: it's the people.

I earn money from YouTube. I monetized my videos right when I hit 1000 subscribers. Although I cannot give exact numbers, on average, a review takes three to four hours to produce (scripting, filming, editing, and uploading). Combine that average amount of time with the average views on a video and I make roughly $1 an hour. That definitely isn't enough to justify my time.

My style depends on the review. If I am extremely excited about the yoyo, or if know I will be able to make a funny video out of the review, it shows. Mostly I try to stay calm and measured in my reviews. I maintain enough speed and excitement to keep the viewer engaged. I try to act as normal and true to myself as I can on camera, while still sounding professional.

I normally follow a structure for my videos, but lately I have been trying to mix things up. As a result, some of my older videos definitely follow this structure, but some newer ones may not. Here it is:

- *I introduce myself and the yoyo*
- *A cinematic sequence with cool music to get the viewer excited*
- *A little about the history and background behind the yoyo*
- *The unboxing experience if the yoyo is special in any way*
- *The specs/pricing/dimensions/material of the yoyo*
- *A look around the yoyo which includes a specs analysis, thoughts on the color, finish, shape, and cup*
- *The feel of the yoyo on the string, how it handles various tricks (fast, slacks, whips, tech tricks, horizontal, binds, regens)*
- *comparing the feel to another yoyo*
- *How the yoyo performs for various grinds (finger, palm, talon, thumb, fingerspin)*
- *I like to conclude the review with any personal opinions*

That's it!

Yoyo Joe's videos don't just provide information for potential yoyo buyers; they also bring new people into the hobby. Someone stumbling across one of his videos can't help but catch his enthusiasm!

Michael "Simply Mike" Washington

Michael's style stands out against other yoyo reviewers. Where Thomas shoots his videos in a single take with as few edits as possible, Mike adds production value. His smooth jazz voice layered over photos of the yoyo can border on hypnotic. I've especially enjoyed his Rain City Skills videos. I include Lego figures with most of my releases, so he starts his reviews of my throws with a little skit using them. It's delightful! He started yoyo reviews for the same reason as Dylan:

> I first got into reviewing because there wasn't much good content on YouTube for the yoyos I was interested in. The few that were on were 'Taking Head' videos. I'm more interested in the feel, playability, and other things besides just your take on things. I try to provide information as well as entertainment while reviewing. What motivates me now is the creativity I can bring to each video. I try not to repeat myself.
>
> I have never made any money off the videos. I've never even monetized my channel. I feel I can use/pull whatever resources into my videos without too much drama because I'm not trying to make money off of someone else's work. My videos and the music, clips, and other things are purely for the fun.
>
> My style? It's called The Art of Fighting without Fighting.
>
> No. I play a slightly exaggerated version of my own real personality. But I watch other reviewers and other types of reviews and insert what is interesting as the need arises.
>
> My format includes a beginning, a body, and an end. There's great variety in those three elements but structurally? That's it. There are some staples that kind of make my videos unique. I show the yoyo spinning in a type of title card sequence. I try to create anticipation for the next video by telling what the next one will be. Overall, I'm trying to be interesting. I think that makes for a better video. And lastly, I've never really made the videos about the yoyo itself. I theme my videos. It's about the theme. The yoyo is the star, not the story.
>
> I love being creative. I get inspired for a particular throw and just go with it. It's an intoxicating feeling. The worst part is when

people declare one reviewer is better than another. We each have a voice, so there is no better, just different.

The popularity of a particular subject affects views. Some videos that I thought would hit, didn't. But getting a popular throw up first counts too.

I've had a couple people run up to me at yoyo events and it was a little shocking. I tell them, 'Internet fame isn't real' [and] we laugh and share a moment. It's so much fun.

I met Mike for the first time at the 2019 World Yoyo Contest in Cleveland. He's as delightful in person as he is online, if not more so. That's one of the joys of attending events—online people resolve into real live humans! I look forward to enjoying Mike's future videos.

Chapter 12: The Videographer

Yoyo is a visual sport. It's difficult to describe in writing, and pictures only say so much. Anyone with a cell phone can film themselves or others showcasing a trick or two. The craft of creating an edited video that holds the attention of the viewer is a skill unto itself. To pull this off, you need a decent quality camera, a lot of patience, and some editing software. Some mad yoyo skills help. I've seen a lot of mediocre videos in my day—many of which were my own. You need to mix music with camera angles and fades to keep your audience watching past the first 30 seconds. In essence, you are trying to create a movie trailer for yourself (or your subject).

When I started yoyo, the top players released a few videos a year—each a well edited collection of tricks, often three or four minutes long. This is now a lot less common. The long-form video seems less popular today. Instead, "trick circle" or single-trick videos filmed and uploaded with a cell phone are now the norm.

So, why the change? One answer is the onward drive of technology. Social media is a lot friendlier to small bites of information. People can sit through a 30 second video of one trick; a three-minute video of multiple tricks, not so much. I know I'm guilty of watching those longer videos for a minute and then skipping to the next thing.

It takes a lot to craft a new trick and master it well enough to film. Some players spend a month working through various permutations before finalizing a combo. Two new combos a month is about my speed now, and what I do is simple compared to many others. For every successful trick on camera, there were dozens of failed attempts. Ask any yoyoer—a trick you can usually hit 10 out of 10 times becomes near-impossible when the camera is turned on! Thus, a three-minute collection may require hours of filming.

In the following section, you'll meet a few folks who take joy in creating videos for the yoyo community to enjoy.

Rowland Balcom

Yoyo is a small community. It's built on the work of individuals who love to share their art. Rowland Balcom shares why video is such a great medium:

> I have asked myself the question why I do this particular thing in such a tiny niche of a small community. Some say I do it to promote our ever-growing community to the public. Others say I do it to promote myself, my sponsor, and what I offer to the yoyo community. Both are reasons for what I do as a YouTuber and an Instagrammer.

> It all started when I made an Instagram account for the first time. I didn't know what to expect or what opportunities were going to fly my way. The same is true about me starting a YouTube channel. I wanted to have a voice. To help people, promote myself and my friends, and contribute where I can to the diverse hobby of yoyoing.

> I do many things as a YouTuber: reviews, tutorials, trick videos, advice, vlogs, and more. I enjoy filming contests [and] I attend as many as possible. Trick videos and vlogs from the contests help to share insight. To share a first-hand experience of yoyo competitions and the people who attend them. I participate in other aspects of yoyo as well. I compete, collect yoyos, and I yoyo for the fun of it.

Sharing and fun. Excellent reasons to do anything!

CHAPTER 12: **THE VIDEOGRAPHER**

Josh Yee

Josh creates detailed and well edited videos showcasing the essence of the contest experience. When I started yoyoing, his were the videos that best shared the feeling of being at a contest—the stage, the people, and the fun of it all!

I started making yoyo contest videos back around 2008. I wanted to relive the contest experience for myself via video memories. By doing so, I felt I could allow others the experience as well. My videos show the entire event from the beginning to end. Plenty of shots showing the serious competition combined with yoyoers hanging out doing cool tricks. I aim to make my videos entertaining not only for yoyoers, but any online passerby who may come across my clip.

There's a common misconception that you need the best equipment. The highest-level equipment with top quality stabilizers and lenses. I say that this is not the case. I began making videos on a tiny handheld flip style camera that could only take one-minute bursts of footage. While limiting, this helped me develop ideas and skills that honed my skills. Nowadays everyone has a camera of decent quality on them at all times in their phones.

Learning to shoot yoyo contests or individual yoyoers is about perspective. I think, 'Ok I can shoot someone doing a trick head on at body level, but what if I got low to the ground and shot at an angle instead?' The addition of movement and flow around the yoyo player as you record adds a big dynamic effect to a trick. Shooting video of yoyo freestyles on stage is easy. Branching out to capture the action everywhere else is where I get creative. Shots of the sales tables in the back, candid shots of players talking and chilling back. Heck, I got a great clip of a thrower sitting back with headphones on and it added something to the video I produced that day.

Thinking out of the box with your shooting of a solo player makes a video stand out. Ambient captures of the surrounding area combined with close ups of the player putting the yoyo string on their finger draws the eye. Different angles, filming a shot through a mirror. These ideas can take a yoyo video from a simple trick circle into a focused production.

Many today find yoyo video creation less rewarding than it used to be. In the age of Instagram, trick circles and quick shots have taken over in popularity. I say that there is still a special place for full length yoyo videos and recaps. The feeling of seeing a finished production come together is rewarding. Editing, color corrections, transitions, sifting through footage to find the one perfect shot, adding the perfect track. These lead to a released finished piece to the public. The feeling is one that a simple Instagram trick could never give me. No matter how many 'likes' it gets.

I hope that more players experiment with video creation. Some may find their place in the community with this unique art style.

Video editing has never been my strong point. Impatience gets the better of me. After hours of filming five or six combos, I want to get them online right away! Yet when Josh puts together a video, it's more than just a flash in the pan. My videos get viewed once or twice. Well edited videos like Josh's get shared, especially when they showcase more than just the yoyo. A great video puts you there with the yoyoer.

Jordan Blofeld

Jordan views the yoyo world through a camera lens. He films contests and creates player showcase videos. In 2017, he put together a promo video for one of my sponsored players, Luna Harran, that was top notch. I asked him to speak about videography.

"My parents always taught me that sharing the things you love was the best way to show your appreciation. That's why I enjoy making yoyo videos. I see how hard my friends work to get as good as they are, and I want to show the world. Get them the

appreciation they deserve. My philosophy is: yoyos are cool, tricks are cooler, but yoyoers are the coolest.

That was why I do it, but I imagine you want to know how I do it. That's harder to pin down. Sometimes I'll go to a gathering or contest with a plan. I'll make a video of a person or showcase the contest as a whole. Sometimes I don't plan anything and capture something spontaneous. Either way, I bring a camera every time, so I have it, just in case. The camera you use isn't that important. I've put in many hours learning about lighting and composition. With these tools you can make great images and films with any camera.

It's the same as learning new yoyo combos or any new skill. The key to progress is practice, practice, practice! Snap photos with your phone and film anything you find interesting. Document special events in your life (as long as you're not ruining them by doing so). Take as many photos and film as many tricks as you can. This is how you get better at doing it.

With all that in mind, I have some tips to help get you started. Wear dark colours to contrast with the yoyo and the string. Try to keep the background dark too. Film in daylight. Keep the sun behind the camera. If it's overcast, the sun will diffuse the light and let through more UV, making yellow string look even brighter.

An extra benefit of practicing a lot is you end up with a lot of footage and photos. You can use all this content to learn how to edit your photos and videos. It doesn't matter what software you use. The differences between them are where the buttons are. Practice editing your content. Make your photos prettier, make your videos more energetic. It's not cheating. It's about producing the best end results possible.

Most importantly, post them when they're done. It's one thing to think you're getting better, another thing to get some proof. Share often and by the time you're ready to create your masterpiece, you'll have an audience to show it to.

Now you know how to do it, the last thing I need to remind you of is to enjoy it. We don't yoyo for money, we yoyo for fun. We yoyo for the people we meet. We yoyo because it makes us and those around us happier. Do it because you love it.

It's been a few years since I've gone hunting for a nice backdrop for film. I used to carry a video camera everywhere I went and capture tricks in front of interesting backgrounds. I've cut together some passable videos, but lack the patience for detailed video and photo editing. Jordan really nails it with his comment about practice. A lot of success with any skill comes down to practice. If you want to master video creation, spend your hours filming everything. Then, spend more hours mastering your software.

Roland Thomas-Biason

(SLVRANDBLK on YouTube)

Roland is an artist. He has a great eye for what works and what doesn't. He does an amazing job of combining lighting, angles, and backgrounds to grab your eye and hold it. I asked him, "Why video?"

I have always been a very visual person, a kinesthetic/visual learner. That's always helped me see ideas as they happen instead of planning them out beforehand. While I am sifting through footage, I can see in real time what I need to do. The same goes for my thoughts during filming. It's all in the viewfinder so I am able to manipulate the image on the fly and see the effect it's having. It requires less imagination and more critical thinking.

I was drawn to yoyo video by the work of other filmmakers and videographers. They laid the groundwork for the fundamentals of yoyo films. People like Mark Artsuni from yoyoing.ru, Allan Herrera, Alec Campbell, and Piotrek Smietana to name a few. One of the first that floored me in video was Yuji from yoyoing.ru. He packed his videos with personality, beyond the content of the tricks.

The creative process is different for every art form. I can take my camera out to Yoyo Club and film players yoyoing, but lack a trained eye because I haven't put in the practice Roland has.

My creative process is very on the fly and intuitive. The first point of call is filming someone whose tricks I enjoy. Without that it's harder to find the creative edge I need to make them look good. Once I'm out in the field with the person, it's all about using the available environment. If you have low light conditions, then you need to abandon any ideas you had and go with that.

My subject and I walk around and chat and find a cool looking place. I'll try some stuff out, if it doesn't work, then we move on. The people with whom I've worked have always trusted me to make the right decision. I don't pressure anyone or try to say what they should do, just help them relax and enjoy themselves. I do the rest. They trust me, and I trust the viewfinder.

I only have one firm rule—if it looks cool, it is cool. This applies to editing and filming alike. I have no preconceived notions of what is technically acceptable and nor do I care. You wouldn't believe the amount of arguments I've been in over technical jargon and what I'm doing is incorrect. It doesn't matter as long as it looks cool.

That said, it's critical to understand your gear and ability. Understand beforehand how much you can manipulate the footage you've got. This helps inform the shots you go for and helps improve the outcome. If you film something in low light without the right approach, you'll end up with a ton of useless footage. I've ended up with a healthy respect for gear and my ability to use it.

Music is as important as the footage itself. I usually choose this whilst I'm editing, and I chose music that fits the tone of the day. If you go in with the music planned out, I feel that it will limit your creativity. It's also good to have a good appreciation for music, and a lot of options in post. I'm a big music lover and I find it's one of the best parts of the process, it's where the bulk of the emotional content comes from.

Rowland's most technically challenging piece is called "Marionette," which reduces yoyoing to hands, string, and yoyo, set in a black void. Watching it, you wouldn't think he filmed his footage outdoors on an overcast day, but that's the magic of video editing. It's a perfect blend of visual edit, speed manipulation, and layering.

Marionette was the one video that required detailed planning. Inspiration came from realizing I could create the effect. Then I reverse engineered the technique to work the way I wanted. That idea wouldn't have looked as good as it did if I had followed the rules from the technical playbook.

My advice? Don't follow the rules, follow what looks good and jump in the sandbox and have fun, or don't, it's fine either way. Having said that, it is vital that you understand [how] your camera, lighting, and software works. It seems like there are a lot of different ideas about what is important when shooting. But, in my opinion, there aren't.

The absolute most important thing is your lens. It's crucial to everything. The best option for starting out and getting results that look good is picking up a 50mm 1.8 prime lens. The focal length along with a low aperture means that you can get loads of light and have a great shallow depth of field. The latter helps separate the background from the foreground and bring the string into focus. You can purchase an affordable DSLR (Digital Single-Lens Reflex) and that will do the trick. Put most of your money in a good lens.

Editing software is less critical. I've made good videos in iMovie. All that's important here is the ability to edit footage in a timeline and to adjust brightness and contrast. Having something to adjust color contrast is important but not essential. Most programs come with these built in so find something cheap to get started on and then you are away. You'll expand your gear as your understanding grows.

If you've ever seen a professional photographer set up (for instance, on school photo day), you'll see an expensive camera on a tripod surrounded by complex lighting equipment. You aren't going to be packing that around, and neither does Roland. What he does know is how to effectively use natural light.

It's all about getting it right when filming, that's where light comes into play. Light is the single most precious commodity available to a photographer or videographer. Learn how to manipulate light and understand its function in the editing process. You capture those beautiful shots without over- or under-exposing. The best-shot videos never needed much adjustment after filming. Daylight is the most usable and cloud cover provides a free built in diffuser. So on a sunny or overcast day, you'll have everything you need.

One last piece of advice—never be afraid to walk away from an idea if it doesn't look right, it will save you so much heartache in the long run. Also, don't forget to charge your batteries.

Charge your batteries—that's sound advice for any aspect of life! I'll add that it's good to pack around a second memory card. There's nothing like walking for an hour to find the perfect spot only to have your memory card die or fill up.

Chapter 13: The Sponsored Player

There is a lot of crossover between the Sponsored Player and the Competitor, especially at the top level. Championship yoyoers usually have a major brand backing them, providing gear and helping with costs.

Being a serious competitor takes a special mentality. It takes a strong drive to get on stage and be the best of the best. Not everyone is gunning for the top spot. Some love the spotlight (guilty as charged), and others want a platform to share and promote the hobby. No matter their motivation, they put in hours of practice.

You find sponsored players in all walks of yoyo life. With the rise of social media as the dominant advertising force, boutique brands are better able to market directly to customers. "Influencers"—yoyoers that others look to for instruction, inspiration, and information—are as valuable as competitors.

When I was a sponsored player on team MonkeyfingeR Design, I wasn't a serious competitor (yet), but I was a teacher. My value to the team was in drawing new players to the brand through the tricks I taught on YouTube. Brands sponsor players ranging from up-and-coming junior players to experienced players with thousands of followers.

Pretty much every category of yoyoer I've discussed in this book can qualify for sponsorship if they offer one or more of these four things:

1. Regular eye-catching content (from contest winning videos to funny videos of cats and yoyos).

2. A following and a personal brand that brings a customer base.

3. Skills that work behind the scenes to help grow the brand (art, web design, video editing, business management, etc.).

4. A history of successful contest performance.

As a brand owner, I regularly have to field emails along the lines of: "I really like to yoyo and want to join your team. Here is my [social media]. I don't have much yet, but I really want to help promote a brand."

These tend to be younger yoyoers with little understanding of the business. They see that their heroes are sponsored and want to emulate them. I could literally write a book on everything you need to know to get sponsored by a brand, and I'd still be wrong. There is no right answer. Here's how I've selected some players over the years:

1. Application – "Fill out this form, and I'll choose the best match." This has rarely worked out well for me. I usually ended up with players who weren't quite the right match, although there were exceptions.

2. Referral – I like this one. Someone I trust recommends another player who would be a good fit.

3. Random chance – More than once, I've met a yoyoer in person and sponsored them on the spot. I trust my instincts, and this has worked out well.

CHAPTER 13: **THE SPONSORED PLAYER**

---

4. Hunt and peck – In some cases, I might watch someone's videos, track their social media success, and then offer a deal. This is hard, takes a lot of time, and I don't enjoy doing it, but it is one way to be sure you are getting quality.

5. Throw piles of money at the problem – When I ran King Yo Star, we scored a sponsorship deal with USA 5A Champion Jake Elliot by paying for his flight to the World Championship and making him a signature yoyo. This worked short term, but we couldn't afford to keep him.

I'm sure every other brand has their own reason for sponsoring players, and every player has their own unique sponsorship experience. So, I will stop talking and let them take over!

Harrison Lee

I have had the privilege of watching Harrison grow from a raw beginner to a World Championship contender. He's a gifted yoyoer. He thinks about yoyo with a notable layer of complexity. I asked him to share the story of how he got his start, and it's a familiar one:

I have been yoyoing for eight years now. I started when my best friend in sixth grade brought a yoyo to recess one day. He let me try his, and I was instantly hooked. He got all my other friends involved and even some of the teachers. We would have yoyo competitions during recess. It started with the basics: who could do the longest Sleeper, the most rotations of Around the World, the longest Walk the Dog, and the most rocks of Rock the Baby. As we all progressed, we began doing short one-minute freestyles to music and judge each other.

Over time, people began to lose interest [and] moved onto other games and hobbies: Minecraft, Chess, Ultimate Frisbee. I was eventually the last yoyoer standing. I needed to find a community outside of school, where I could practice my yoyo tricks. That is when I discovered the Vancouver Yoyo Club. Everyone had a unique style, and odd yoyos to try. Having a group of experienced throwers I could learn from, practice with, and innovate tricks with was integral [to my] development in yoyoing.

It's funny. I remember the friend that got him hooked on yoyo. He was a member of the Vancouver Yoyo Club but drifted away and left Harrison to keep progressing.

The first yoyo competition that I took part in was the Western Canadian Regional Contest in Vancouver in 2011. At the time I had only been yoyoing for just a couple of months, but I thought I would [take] a shot at competing in the junior division. A few of my other friends were competing as well, so it was a nice excuse to get out of my weekend piano lessons. I entered the contest for fun, with very few expectations of how I would place and ended up walking out with a silver medal. I enjoyed the thrill of competing and performing. That is when I realized that it was something that I should pursue further. Little did I know that it would become a defining part of my identity.

Harrison was a rising star from the get-go. It didn't take him long to surpass the skills of most of the club members. He caught the attention of Canadian Yoyo brand CLYW's owner Chris Mikulin early on, and he's been a great brand ambassador for them over the years. One of the major perks of being a sponsored player with serious skills is a getting "signature" yoyo.

In [2014] I got the opportunity to design my own professional competition-grade yoyo. The Orca project with CLYW was an amazing learning experience. The whole experience exposed me to yoyo design and the business side of yoyoing. I had to master a wide range of concepts and skills. It began with advanced physics and the technical necessities of yoyo design. From there I had to create a marketing strategy for when the yoyo would hit the market and pitch my concept to CLYW. I was the project manager and was responsible for creating a business plan for the manufacturers who would ultimately assemble and sell the yoyo. I created timelines, assigned tasks to my team, and ensured everyone completed their responsibilities on time. My name was attached to a yoyo sold on international markets.

What a great opportunity! Harrison does a great job of highlighting how much work goes into creating an amazing yoyo. He works hard at everything in life, and yoyo is no exception.

The "Orca" was an instant hit, with multiple sold-out international runs. It was considered a breakthrough design, adapting characteristics from the best modern yoyos in the industry, and quickly became a competition favorite!

Dennis Dressel

Dennis Dressel goes by the screen name "Hobbygod" on social media. He spends a fair chunk of his yoyo time sharing tricks with others through his tutorials. He's sponsored by Airetic Strings, so I asked him to share his thoughts on life as a sponsored player.

Rob (the owner of Airetic strings) is an awesome guy that really cares about the community. Visit their website and you will find walk-throughs for people looking to set up their own string rig. They trade strings to give people feedback and help as much as they can. This spoke volumes to me. They're more focused on helping people develop their own strings over selling them. They also make very good product. I wouldn't want to work with a company whose product I don't enjoy.

They offer me a large discount on everything in their store, and in return I represent their brand. They help me through getting me the bearings, pads, and strings I need at a reduced rate. Part of my 'job' as an Airetic representative [is] to bring sample packs of string to contests and let people try them. Many people (like me) have played poly string all their lives and may be a little skeptical of nylon/boutique string. I also represent them in my videos and posts.

Representing a brand adds a layer of work to one's yoyo life. I asked Dennis if he was pursuing a yoyo brand sponsorship in addition to his work with Airetic Strings.

I'd like to be sponsored by a yoyo company one day. I think joining Airetic Strings is a step in the right direction. As my Instagram and YouTube continue to grow, I hope yoyo companies will become interested in me. There are a few companies that I'd like to work with. But I AM interested in a good group of people and a product I enjoy using.

Otherwise, I am content with where I am at in my yoyo career right now. I enjoy creating unique tricks, sharing them, and creating tutorials for the ones that people enjoy and ask for. My girlfriend wants me to compete. So I am working on 2a and looking to compete in a year or two when I feel I am good enough.

He's given himself a challenge. 2a is a hard style to master, but I'm sure he'll get there!

Waylon Crase

I've been friends with Waylon Crase for years now. His behind the scenes contributions are vital to the success of Rain City Skills. Waylon represents the less visible sponsored players, the ones who bring support skills to promotion and marketing.

Have you always wanted to be a sponsored yoyo player but lack the requisite skill, talent, expertise, outgoing personality, and good looks? Have I got some news for you! You can still get sponsored! Keep reading to find out how!

Seriously. You can be sponsored without being a great player. There are plenty of people out here who beg the question, 'How is this guy on a team?' I'm one of them. I'm going to try to explain my personal path to sponsorship in a concise way, despite the convoluted steps that got me to where I am now.

I am currently sponsored by both Rain City Skills and MonkeyfingeR Vines. Prior to them, I was sponsored by BigYoyo String then YoyoZeekio. Pretty miraculous for a guy who has, like, two good tricks in his repertoire. I achieved this through being visible, available, enthusiastic, and useful.

BigYoyo String offered me a spot after I did a series of boutique string reviews on the YoYoExpert forums just for fun. I had no ambitions in mind while writing the reviews. It was just an effort to participate in the community and an additional way to enjoy the hobby. David 'Shyguy' Lopez was on the team as well. When BigYoyo String closed up shop a year or so later, Shyguy had picked up a sponsorship at YoyoZeekio and helped in getting me added to the team.

During that time, I became significantly more visible. I went to contests and shared product around, fielded loads of questions through social media, helped with some of the marketing, scouted for new team members, tested new products, and more.

One afternoon, I was chatting with Jeremy McKay online and suggested some idea or other for Rain City Skills. He thought it was funny and joked he should poach me from YoyoZeekio. Turns out, he wouldn't have to. Mitch disbanded the team and Jeremy immediately offered me a lucrative contract to exclusively play with RCS yoyos. I declined the lucrative bit and offered to work for him in exchange for circus peanuts (the gross orange kind) and having temper tantrums regularly directed at me by His Lordship (that's what Jeremy makes the team call him. We're also not allowed to make direct eye contact with him when in person).

I'm kidding, of course. His Lordship takes good care of His team.

At RCS, I mostly help with marketing and work behind the scenes, where I belong. So far I've: named several colorways, named at least one yoyo, helped construct the signature RCS unboxing experience, created the graphic designs used on stickers and shirts and engravings, vended at contests, managed the logistics for the Boutique Yoyo Collective, tested prototypes, and a bunch of other little things that would take way too long to type out. And now that I'm looking at this list, I'm thinking we may need to revisit the lucrative portion of my contract.

The point to all this is—none of what I contribute to a company has anything to do with my skill as a yoyo player. But I have other skills. You may be in the same boat. You may be passionate about the hobby, driven, filled with a desire to help shape a brand and be a part of something special. Don't be afraid to put yourself out there. Don't be afraid to be visible. Companies need people like you.

The path to sponsorship isn't always a direct one and it's not always the same path for everyone. Mine certainly wasn't. I wouldn't have gotten here any other way.

Waylon has been a most effective minion, and I've been a very kind and generous sponsor. Don't believe a word he says to the contrary.

Connor Seals

Connor Seals is one of the top players in North America. He's talented and works very hard. He's sponsored by SF, a yoyo brand focused on competitive yoyos for competitive players. Connor is a competitive person, so I asked him to talk a bit about sponsorship and what drives him to compete.

I'm sponsored by SF Yoyos, I love it! My job is to promote their products through social media and contest performance. Their job is to give me products and provide monetary compensation. This usually comes in the form of hotel rooms and plane tickets as well as yoyo royalties. There are so many benefits about SF Yoyos...They pay for my flights and hotel (at least most of it). But also, I get to be on the most fun team. We all have such a great relationship and they're all such good yoyoers, but most of all, good people. Our Facebook chat is always flooded with jokes and conversation and yoyo tricks. SF has given me my first opportunity at having a signature yoyo, which releases later this year. I'm really excited!

A basketball player loves competition and loves basketball. A hockey player loves competition and loves hockey. I love competition, and LOVE yoyoing. Sports and competition have always been a big part of my life. I was a state champ cross-

country runner in high school and have learned that consistency over time makes champions.

When I started competing [at] yoyo in 2012, I knew if I practiced consistently, I could be a champion. I love the process of making a freestyle, I love performing and I love yoyoing. But the only thing that keeps bringing me back to the stage is my love of competition.

A yoyoer is an athlete. Repetitive motion injuries are common, and like any athlete, the competitive yoyoer must take care of their body and mind. The focus needed is intense. Connor is planning a year in advance before his next big competition, to make sure he has the most time to practice and the best shot at victory.

A new goal that I'm setting right now is [to] win US Nationals 2020 and the World Yoyo Contest in 2020. In my eyes there's no better time for me to do it. I have slowly worked my way up the Nationals placements, taking second [place] in Nationals this year. Evan Nagao is no longer competing, which means a HUGE chunk of competition no longer is there. Evan even agreed to help me construct my world winning freestyle!

I need to balance out my trick difficulty, use a song that everybody recognizes, have an innovative performance, and practice a lot! I want to have the freestyle finished by January 2020. Then I can practice it all year and perform the freestyle to large groups of people many times before Nationals. Gentry Stein, Zach Gormley, and Evan Nagao are three legendary players from the US (and the only National Champions since 2012). I think it's time for a player to take that spot as a new US National Champion (and World Champion)!

When I'm practicing for a contest, I will try to practice 6-12 hours a week. I will either practice one hour, two hours, or take a day off. I never want to overdo it because this year I've been getting pains in my shoulder and forearm. Practice begins with a run-through of my tricks without music a good number of times before I include music. I never stop a run-through with music so I can practice recovering from mistakes.

A fixed goal for the contest helps me focus. Win? That's not specific enough. How do I want to win? What message do I want to give with the freestyle? Who is in the audience? Is it mostly yoyo players? If so, have a more direct focus on trick content and impressiveness. Is the venue more public? Focus more on performance and entertainment for the non-yoyo player. Serious or happy music? Etc. After I choose the music, I edit it and build tricks to fit the music.

My philosophy is: how can I make this song better with yoyo tricks? Is the song groovy? How can I make it groovier? Is it intense? How can I build tension in the room? Etc. When choosing tricks, no matter what freestyle I do, I try to have as much trick variety as I can. Because most good songs also have variety.

I asked Connor what his pre-game routine looks like. How does one prepare for a yoyo contest? So much of one's success on stage comes down to mental preparation and focus.

I always try to chill and not think about what could go wrong, but what will go right. Before I step on stage, I run through the routine for maybe 20-30m to warm up and feel comfortable. I always keep extra strings in my pocket in case I need to do a quick string switch shortly before walking on stage. I run through my freestyle during the competitors before me. When their music starts, I start my music and go. I pretend I'm onstage. This is often backstage or close to the stage so I can feel the energy of the audience after every run-through.

I don't try to suppress nervousness but accept it and acknowledge the audience and be professional. Pretending the audience doesn't exist is never a good idea. They exist. Perform!"

I asked Connor to share any advice he had for others.

"If you've been yoyoing for one year, two years, or even up to four or five years, don't get too frustrated if you're not the best yoyo competitor. Just learn to enjoy yoyo! I didn't win my first contest until six years of yoyoing. When I compete, I treat failure as an opportunity. I try to analyze how I could improve and come back better every time. The biggest challenge I had on stage was in 2014 at the IL state 1a Prelims. The yoyo string slipped off my finger and the 1a yoyo flew off the stage towards the judges! I switched yoyos and still made finals somehow!

I've been a competitor, although nowhere near Connor's level. A pair of car accidents forced me to back off, but I didn't let it stop me. Physically limited to 15-20 minutes of practice a day, I kept my time concentrated on targeted practice. Doing this for two years without missing a day took me to my first Canadian Championship. It's hard work daily. You need to put in the time and focus. Competing isn't for everyone, but there is no feeling quite like the lights and the stage and a cheering crowd. Connor's story leads us into the next section of the book – The Competitor.

Chapter 14: The Competitor

On the opposite end of the spectrum from the Hobbyist is the Competitor. Odds are that the idea of serious competitive yoyoing is a new one for you. Yet it is a growing sport with a dedicated following. Take a moment to search "World Yoyo Champion" on YouTube. The level of athleticism, skill, and professionalism is intense. Competitive yoyoers with an eye on a title spend hours each day training and studying the competition. They build tricks and routines that will score well and impress the judges. The competitor lives for the sport, much like an NBA basketball player or professional figure skater.

I've talked to many competitors over the years. I've been one. Everyone has a different system of practice and training. Becoming World Champion was never a reasonable goal for me. Becoming a Canadian Champion was more achievable. Even that required years of daily practice. Each competitor develops their own style, although some types of trick combination score better than others. It's not enough simply to have the fastest or the most complex tricks. Competitors are also scored on their performance as a whole.

For instance: Are they showing professionalism on stage? Is their routine choreographed to the music? Do they engage the audience? How much variation have they included during their two- to three-minute routine? Too many similar tricks during a performance mean your score drops. Some competitors choose to master high-risk tricks; these tricks take more time to set up, and if the performer makes a mistake, they end up with a tangled mess of string. Other competitors choose fast-paced and complex tricks; these tricks have less risk of failure when taken on their own, but when combined in a series, they require near-perfect execution.

Being a serious competitor takes a special mentality—a drive to get on stage and be the best of the best. Not everyone is gunning for the top spot. Some love the spotlight (guilty as charged) and others want a platform to share and promote the hobby. No matter their motivation, they put in hours of practice. Years ago, I asked World 5a Champion, Jake Elliot, why he stopped competing. He confided that attaining the level of perfection needed for the title was a full-time job—on top of school and actual paying work. There is a big difference between yoyoing for fun and practicing a routine or perfecting a trick. Players that create videos have the flexibility of stopping the camera and re-shooting the trick as many times as it takes. The competitor has to get it right the first time, every time.

Gentry Stein

Two-time World Champion Gentry Stein is one of the most focused individuals I've ever met. He operates from a very driven, "eyes on the prize" attitude that has served him well. For Gentry, failure was never an option. He's all about determination and perseverance, and is known for his carefully choreographed routines. Any aspiring champion needs to know the rules inside and out so they can plan the best way to score. Gentry studies the stage like a golfer studying the green, mapping it out and planning every detail of his performance.

> I started yoyoing when I was eight years old. I loved sports and art. I found that yoyo was a medium that allowed me to pursue both my competitive and creative nature. I started to take yoyoing seriously in middle school. In 2009 I entered my first competition, a regional in San Francisco. I ended up getting 15th place in the

finals and was very disappointed with the result. That's when I started to put serious work in.

February 2010, I took second place at a regional in Seattle. That's where it all took off. The following year, I took third at the World Yoyo Contest, less than a point away from winning. I continued to develop for a couple years. I entered the 2013 World Yoyo Contest with confidence that I would leave with the world title. I approached the stage for my semi final with confidence but left the stage in disappointment after a sloppy performance. I remember reading through the results list of finalists, and my name was absent. I had an intense emotional mix of despair and motivation. I felt like I wanted to quit. But at the same time there was no doubt in my mind. I would become the 2014 World Yoyo Champion.

Fast forward to the next year. I changed my approach, broadened my strategy, and came into the contest more prepared than ever. This time, my name was at the top of the semi finals results list. Chills ran throughout my body as I landed the last trick of my finals performance. The audience in Prague was impeccable, with too much energy to describe. The chills come back every time my mind wanders back to the memories. Hearing the MC announce my name for first place was one of the most rewarding moments of my life.

I was in that audience and remember the energy. The noise from the audience was palpable.

So, what happens after you win? What do you do with your newfound fame? Gentry has a great answer: Use it to spread the love of yoyo.

As a World Champion, I am now considered an ambassador. I have traveled to promote yoyo in over 15 different countries. I've been featured on television shows and starred in the music video for the single 'Strings' by the band 'Baby Raptors.' I proved you don't need to spend a ton to be the champion when I won the US Nationals with a $16 YoyoFactory Replay. I had many more *incredible experiences that all stemmed from this passion. My goal of changing what people think to be possible with a yoyo continues. I'm incredibly excited to keep pushing the boundaries of creation as well as inspiring others to follow their own passion.*

Gentry continues to maintain a high profile. He travels the world as an official rep for the brand YoyoFactory, doing what yoyoers always do— amazing a crowd and finding those special few who will pick up a yoyo and lead the next generation of champions.

Evan Nagao

Diet and hydration are important with any type of performance. Consuming pop, chips, and candy the night before a competition can leave your mind and body weak. Compare an Olympian from 100 years ago with one today. The skill levels are very different. A big piece of the puzzle is the huge advances that have been made in the area of health science. Any professional athlete or trainer will tell you to eat well and keep hydrated. A yoyoer needs to do the same. It's easy to forget that your hands don't operate alone; every muscle in your body works together to hit that perfect yoyo routine.

I asked two-time USA National Champion and 2018 World Champion Evan Nagao to share his training and contest prep strategy.

Before a contest, there's a certain routine I follow. First, I always make sure that if I plan to win, I start preparing my routine at least three to six months in advance. I'll practice every day [for] about four hours, constantly upgrading the routine until it's optimized. Once I'm there, I hardly practice the day of finals. The reason is because it's easy to burn yourself out, as I have many times in the past. I trust that all the practice that I'd been doing is enough and allow my muscle memory to do the rest.

About three hours before the contest is where my preparation gets quite nuanced. I eat a 12" subway sandwich with lots of veggies, turkey, salami, mayo, and mustard on wheat bread. I also eat a few leaves of lettuce if I can find a grocery store near the venue. Then exactly one hour before I perform, I do three sets of what's called 'Wim Hof Breathing,' which floods my body with oxygen. This helps me clear my mind and gets me into peak state. Then 30 minutes before I go on, I practice my routine non-stop. This is to keep my body warm. In my experience, practicing any more will burn me out and any less will make me cold.

When it's my turn next, I head to the back of the stage where I practice the first tricks in my routine. Also, if anyone is there, I try to make small talk, asking them who they are and such to get myself out of my head. In the case of US Nationals, I ended up talking with Graeme Stellar, the MC.

The rush of being in front of a crowd is why I compete. Evan has been a performing yoyoer since he was old enough to hold a yoyo. He has the dedication and skill it takes to be a true champion and a well-grounded attitude towards the time on stage.

I make sure to smile and acknowledge the audience. Your showmanship score is influenced by how you enter and exit the stage. It's important to be on top of your game even before the music starts. My goal is to create the best experience I can give. It's not about hitting my routine clean, nor is it to score the most points in tech and evals. I practiced over three months to do these things.

Once I'm on stage, the only thing that matters is making sure the audience is loving it. I particularly focus on smiling a lot, and if I miss a trick, make sure the crowd knows that it's okay, and motion for them to keep cheering.

I think paradoxically, it's this carefree attitude that allows you to actually go clean. If you care too much about yourself, or how you'll do in the contest, you'll make yourself anxious and have a hard time hitting your tricks. It's a catch-22.

Once I'm done, I make sure the audience and the judges know that I just won the contest or at least that I felt I won. Even though your routine is over, they are writing their evaluation scores. You can still influence the numbers. I always thank the spectators,

*and in my head, I actually say 'Thank you for being an amazing
audience.' Then I walk off stage and celebrate with my friends.*

It's so easy to stress yourself out on stage. One mistake can derail a
routine. My best advice for a new competitor is always, "When you smile,
you trick your brain into thinking everything is OK."

Evan treats his championship status the same way Gentry does—as an
opportunity to give back. He explains:

*As one of the top competitors on the scene, it's impossible to not
have some level of influence. For someone in this position, it's
always important to realize the responsibility that comes with it.
I try my best to create peace within the community and help keep
our culture wholesome and enjoyable.*

*I believe part of winning big titles comes with a responsibility to
push yoyoing forward. If you win a big contest, and do nothing
to grow the sport, you have not fulfilled your full responsibilities
as the Champion (in my opinion). I've done press releases and
appeared on large media outlets to spread the word. There's only
going to be one [World] Champion each year, so if the opportunity
to grow yoyoing isn't taken, then it's wasted.*

After the 2019 World Championship, Evan announced that he was
finished with competition. He's not done with yoyo, but he's done with the
daily grind that keeps you on the cutting edge of competition play. He still
loves yoyo, but he also has time now for his other hobbies, such as writing
and singing songs! In 2019, he released the single "Waves." It's on YouTube,
so be sure to check it out!

Connor Scholten

Connor Scholten is one of those rare players who compete in multiple
divisions. What does this mean? To understand, take the amount of work
that Gentry and Evan describe, then double or triple it. Connor shares
a story of the dedication and determination that goes into becoming a
champion. Don't try this at home, kids.

*The weekend before the 2014 US Nationals, I started getting sick
while performing a Vaudeville show in Cleveland. I didn't detect
the flu-like symptoms until we were on the road home. That*

Monday I felt like my entire immune system was being attacked and no part of my body was without pain. I got a prescription at Urgent Care and spent every waking moment the next few days in bed. I hoped to curtail the symptoms to no avail. I decided, against all the advice of sane people, to still tag along on the planned trip. Though I looked like death, I was unwilling to wait another year to attempt a national title.

This trip set in stone already took a grueling scenic route. I had to drive across Michigan, pick up people enroute to Detroit International, layover in Seattle, then Portland to pick up more people. Packed into a full vehicle, it was 10 more hours through Oregon and into Chico California to arrive late the night before the contest. Total travel time from home to Chico took 36 hours with a temperature change of 60°F (15.5°C) to around 100°F (37.7°C). According to the contest schedule that year, I would compete in 2a mid-afternoon on the outdoor stage. The other divisions, including my 4a entry, competed inside the theater that night.

Mixing medication, energy drinks, (and a little denial), I psyched myself into showcasing an energetic 2a routine. Unable to take my full liquid prescription past airport security, I timed the last of my medication for that routine. Combined with the sugar crash and heat exhaustion I passed out right after leaving the stage. I forgot where I was twice during the routine but managed a well executed performance.

The awards for 2a were presented straight away due to a schedule change and I received second [place]. I was devastated. With emotions and various pains festering, I made the decision while lying on the sidewalk to enter 4a that night. After drifting from the park to the theater I kept trying to stand up and practice for three minutes at a time. I tried this because my preparation the week of Nationals got thrown out of whack.

Long story short, I [had not created] my 4a routine yet. I previously created trick sequences [and] picked a song, but had *no choreography. I hadn't even attempted the tricks to music. My body gave out again and again. I collapsed on the entrance ramp to the auditorium in front of people.*

Out of options and time, all I could do was make the routine using my imagination. I listened to the song while lying down an hour before the big moment, piecing all my premade combos in my head like a jigsaw puzzle. Hoping the routine I envisioned would work, I wrote down my plan.

This time, I did not leave it to chance and called on the help of my teammate, Jake Elliott. He knew my tricks, so we created a signal system with baseball-like gestures so he could tell me what to do next during the performance. We were not sure if this would work. No one has ever tried this before since most other players do not cram.

In a theater of a couple thousand, Jake was the only one standing up in the corner of the front row, notes in hand, ready to feed me signals. The moment arrived, [and] I concentrated on two things—stay standing and complete the trick. I was calm in the moment and did not worry what was next. Between tricks, there is a small window between catching and throwing the yoyo where my eyes could glance at Jake. Every time I looked, I had no idea what was next, but Jake's ridiculous poses triggered my memory every time. The system worked brilliantly. Together, we executed the best Offstring routine I ever performed. Albeit it not perfect.

One of my drops sent my yoyo rolling to the back corner near a lighting post with a base of razor-sharp edges. My favorite trick involved using my feet which meant I was in socks with no shoes. So when I tripped and kicked the metal plate it cut my big toe open. I didn't even realize it happened until a couple hours after when the sound system vibrated the floor and I felt a funny

*tingling sensation. I looked at the blood-soaked sock and slowly
figured it out.*

*So off to the emergency room again. A nurse administered
antiseptic, peeled my skin back into place, and gave me a tetanus
shot. All the while I am texting trying to figure out my 4a placing.
It wasn't until I arrived back at the hotel someone told me it was
4th.*

*In the years that followed, I continued my pursuit of the
national title. My experiences were a little less intense but still
unrelenting. Finally I would summit the 2a title in 2017. I would
like to think this is the type of willpower it takes to win a top-level
yoyo competition. That each champion player in my situation
would have made these same decisions without hesitation. Okay,
maybe not all of them.*

"I passed out right after leaving the stage"—if that isn't high-level
dedication, I don't know what is. The closest I've been to that level of
dedication was sustaining a bloody knee from sliding across the stage to
save a runaway yoyo. To drive across the country with a full-blown flu is a
whole different level of determination. His masterful knowledge of his tricks
allowed him to build his routine in his mind, and his ability to visualize and
prepare his failing body finally carried him to victory.

Chapter 15: Women in Yoyo

I asked a writer friend of mine, Susan, to review an early draft of this book. She read and read, and then said, "I like where this book is going. But I have to ask, where are all the women? There must be female yoyoers." I answered that there are lots of women out there yoyoing. Yet the visible ones are few and far between. Yoyo is a hobby that is male dominated. My Instagram stats generally show around 90% of my viewers are male(those statistics don't include non-binary individuals) .

I asked some female-identified yoyoers to talk about yoyos. We talked about the day-to-day basics of yoyo, the community, and the women-only freestyle division of competitions. Some of their stories fit best in other places in this book. This section highlights a few stories that relate specifically to the experience of being a woman in yoyo.

Abby Brodsky

Abby Brodsky is a seasoned veteran of the yoyo scene. She is an international competitor and an advocate for women in yoyo. I told her about my book, and she offered to share her experience. Abby gives us a cross section of her experiences throughout the yoyo world. She speaks of getting her start and finding a community within yoyo:

Being a girl in yoyoing is interesting. I mean when I went to my first contest, I was the only girl there competing. It was a culture shock. My mom thought I would quit after that. Especially considering I thought I'd meet other girls at a contest and there weren't [any].

Girls seem to find the hobby and enjoy it, but when they find the lack of girls in the community, they either quit yoyoing or choose not to be involved in the community. It can be great to be a girl in yoyo because you can encourage other yoyo girls to join. However, it can also be lonely if you're not in a 'yoyo dense' area.

There are also some logistical issues. Like you know how guys can room together for a yoyo contest to split costs and such? Well, it's a lot harder for a yoyo girl to do that. I either have to find another girl to room with or share with a bunch of boys. If you're young like me (I'm 19 right now) that takes a lot of convincing [with] your family members. This makes it hard to go to other contests.

Even though I talk about how great it is to be a girl yoyoing in the community, there are downsides. In Asia many of the girls that yoyo are over sexualized and used as a selling point with the yoyos. They are expected to pose and be 'cute' with them. Also, it can be kind of awkward. Some guys you talk to at contests are too socially awkward to talk to a yoyo girl or say something completely off putting.

It's also very welcoming. The yoyo community is tight knit, so imagine the yoyo girl community. Everyone knows everyone and is supportive of each other. Like at 2018 US Nationals, Talia, Kira, and I were three peas in a pod and almost always talking to each other and supporting each other on stage. We would get lunch and dinner together to take a break from all the guys.

When you are a yoyo girl, you also get a lot of support from other girls online. On social media this is common because we all follow each other and offer support. Like before I had an Instagram, I would make YouTube videos and right now about one-tenth are girl yoyoers. We all subscribe to and comment on each other's videos and posts. We like to encourage each other.

So, when someone catches wind of a girl picking up yoyoing, I follow and keep encouraging them to yoyo. When you're a girl, it's important to have a presence online so you can encourage others. It's also surprisingly easy to get sponsored. A solid quarter of all the yoyo girls I know of are sponsored because companies want girls to get into yoyos.

It's great to hear that there is so much support among women in the community. While she's encountered some challenges, Abby has found far more joy in her chosen hobby.

Jennifer Baybrook

Jennifer Baybrook is the only woman to hold the title of World Champion (not including the Women's Division). She won her title in 1998, so I asked her to share some thoughts on life as a woman who became the best yoyoer in the world.

Growing up, my father made me mad because he was old-fashioned and treated women as not equal. To him, the man always had the final word. But I was a bit rebellious and determined to prove that women were equal. I did not want to be as good as the boys, I needed to be better. I tried to not stand out as a girl but be one of the boys.

For me, it was a good time to be a girl in the scene. I proved myself as serious, focused, and tough as anyone. I worked hard to earn that acceptance as part of the group. I was never a girl, I was Jen. Over the years, I had other girls ask me how they could get the boys to treat them better or with more respect. The boys did not look at them as good players, but as 'good for a girl.'

My response? Earn their respect.

If you do not want them to say you're 'good for a girl' then you need to be better than they are, or at the least train harder and let them see that. No matter what in life, as women, we will continue to face that challenge. Women that rise to the top in a male-dominated field do it by training/working harder and pushing themselves to do more.

I cannot imagine the frustration of needing to be better to be treated as an equal. That might be one reason the organizers of the 2014 World Championships created a separate Women's Division. I asked Jennifer to share some highlights from her life as a yoyoer. Aside from her competition life, Jennifer was also a touring yoyo performer and promoter.

Definitely winning the Nationals and Worlds [was a highlight]. I think Nationals was more memorable for me because I entered with this amazing calm feeling that I would win it. It was not 'I could or maybe I would,' it was 'I'm going to win this.' Completing the compulsories and my first freestyle with zero mistakes thrilled me. The moment when everyone ran up to me saying 'Wow you just did a clean freestyle' or 'You know you just won this?'

When I was competing, I was always in this zone where I somehow blocked everything out that was going on around me. I also never watched other freestyles. I stayed in my zone visualizing and practicing my routine. If you walk off that stage only remembering the beginning, middle, and end you did good.

Beyond the competitions, the best moments had to be all the world trips and fun moments with the team members of THP (Team High Performance). There are too many amazing ones to know where to start. I also remember all the fans and the friends that I made along the way. It is so humbling to have so many kids look up to me and want to just shake my hand, give me a hug or present me with a special gift. They would follow us around until they could snap a picture. We would have fans chasing or cheering for us and wanting everything signed.

Yet I would go back home to my simple life and a small house that my parents had, and it would all seem so surreal. It was like we were these rock stars with trading cards, commercials, and nonstop TV & magazine interviews. But behind the curtain I lived a simple life with parents that struggled with basic living expenses. Our house was simple, we never had a lot. At school I was this eccentric girl with poor parents. But when on the road and at competitions I became somebody completely different.

I finished up by asking Jen if she still yoyos. She shares:

I went into marketing for about 10 years after college. I worked my way up to a successful senior level management position and then I quit and changed fields completely. During my corporate days I realized I missed interacting with people and motivating them

So, I found a field doing something I love and a field that allows me to help people change their lives. I shifted to personal training and coaching. I still do yo-yo presentations occasionally and I've always stayed in touch with the friends I made during this time. I will eventually write a blog or a book about my life and the unusual journey I had.

I would happily read that book! Jennifer's World Championship video is available on YouTube and is worth a watch. The sport has changed since her time, but the passion and dedication she had for the sport is still front and center. If you want to learn more about her, she's been sharing some of her story on the blog section of the Ducan Yoyo website.

Stephanie Haight

Stephanie has been an active yoyoer for many years. She was a rep for team YoYoJam, one of the bigger brands in the yoyo world in the early 2000's. I asked her to share her experience of getting started in yoyo.

My experience starting out in the yoyo community was much different from most other female players. Before getting into yoyoing, I always hung out with the boys or did things that girls my age weren't doing. I found contests or club meets intimidating at first. Not because of my gender, but because of my skills.

I grew up with the mindset that I needed to be as good as everyone else and to prove it as well. The number of guys who wanted to talk to me because I'm a female yoyoer surprised me. I got so much support. At the time I started yoyoing, Ann Connelly was the only well-known female competitor in the states. Because of that, people encouraged me to keep going.

I raised a question I'd seen in online discussions: Why have a separate division for women? Gender isn't a consideration for contest entry, although female yoyoers in the top ranks are rare in world competition history. Stephanie says:

I can see both sides to why or why not the division exists, but personally I see it being more beneficial than not. Seeing girls in the division showed me how much the female yoyo community [has grown] since I started back in 2010. Although some of these players now 'own' the contest scene, it's good to have a division to show that girls are now in the game.

I do think it is the easiest time in yoyoing for girls to join, so I am unsure of how much longer the division is necessary. The World Contest has an Over-40 Division for fun, so the Women's Division is similar. It's a great way for the female players to get together and be with one another.

It's great to hear that it's easier for girls and women to get involved in yoyo these days. In my experience running yoyo clubs in schools, there isn't a lack of interest! Kids love to yoyo no matter who they are! I like the idea that we live in a time when yoyoing is open to everyone.

Visible role models are important, and the Women's Division provides a showcase and a spotlight for these role models. The more you can see people like you doing things you want to do, the more confidence you have to push forward in a community. The yoyo community is one that thrives on variety and innovation. I like to think we welcome anyone who wants to play.

Chapter 16: The Trick Innovator

Yoyo is a hobby, sport, and art form. Every modern yoyo trick "combo" comprises little pieces learned from others. Once you learn the basics, it's hard not to want to take those bits and rearrange them. More often than not, you'll find your early attempts to create tricks aren't new. As you develop, however, things get more interesting. This chapter is a tour through some of the most creative minds in yoyo—from Hobbyist yoyoers who create their own tricks to Innovators who change the game.

The terms "trick," "element," and "combo" pop up frequently in this section. Let's take a second to go over what these terms mean. Traditionally, a "trick" was what you could do in the 10-15 seconds while your fixed-axle yoyo spun. With ball bearings, we have more time. So, instead of a single trick, we talk about "elements" (individual interactions of string and yoyo) put together into "combos." Where it can get confusing is that these combos are also referred to as tricks. While the two terms arguably have different meanings, it's easiest to treat "trick" and "combo" as synonymous.

"Styles" of yoyo refers to the many ways to play with a yoyo—not different tricks, but different setups. See Appendix B for a full, if not complete, list.

For **Nicolas Lotman**, innovation requires the right creative headspace. He says:

> To create a yoyo trick, I need to be in a certain mood. Once I'm there, I take the yoyo and start from different mounts. If I find an element I like, I try to tie it in to other elements. I want the trick to flow nicely, but most importantly to feel good when I do it.

Kent Ampoon takes pieces of what he sees and shuffles them around until he has a new combo!

> I make my own tricks by getting elements or movements from other players. I try to imitate what they are doing, but either in a different mount or making a trick in the same mount. I figure out a way to progress the combo by messing around with the mount. Eventually I find something new. Then I combine it with other combos. If the trick starts with a trapeze, I find a stylish way to get into a trapeze.

Drago Moore voices the shared frustration involved in creating new tricks:

> If you ask any modern yoyoer, we've all had the moment of frustration. We mess around, end up somewhere awesome, then spending an hour trying to get back to that place.
>
> I watch and learn other peoples' tricks. I pick apart elements you can swap into another trick and attempt to put them together in a new way. Then cry when it binds on me accidentally, cry when it hits my face, and cry when I land it because it'll be at least another ten fails before you get it again. The creation of a combo is always worth the frustration.

Many recreational yoyoers spend their time like Nicolas, Drago, and Kent. We work to build combos out of the pieces we've learned. At my level, it's likely that someone else in the world has come up with a similar combination. Still, that doesn't invalidate our achievement. In fact, the opposite is true. It's pretty cool finding someone throwing a similar combo to one of yours! I sometimes wonder if there is a hive mind of yoyoers spanning the globe.

Italian yoyoer **Ricardo Fraolini** is a talented yoyoer. While he is capable of crafting top level competition combos, he is better known for unexpected, less complex, but equally challenging tricks. I asked him what defines a trick innovator. He explains:

> I define an innovator as someone with the ability to think out of the box and find new moves, mounts, and concepts. I'm thrilled when people tell me 'I learned that trick from you' or "Here's a variation of your move'; I'm very honored to inspire someone. I have so many good memories and it's hard to choose one! With yoyoing I found some of the best friends I have, and I traveled in a lot of crazy places! The hobby changed my life for the better, I will always be thankful to the toy!

Ricardo's Instagram account is indeed inspiring. Watching his videos tickled my brain and made me think about techniques I wasn't using. He's also someone who fits into the Teacher category, with a YouTube channel sharing tutorials of several of his trick concepts with the world.

The following pages highlight a handful of innovators like Ricardo. These are players who go places no one has gone, or take what others are doing and twist and shape it into something fresh. There are many types of trick creators. Some create tricks for the average yoyoer. Their creations are inspiring, but still make sense to most yoyo players. On close inspection, we can tell what they are doing, even if we couldn't imagine having created such a trick. Luna Harran and Zammy are players who think so far outside of the box that even the most skilled players have a hard time following them.

Luna Harran

Luna Harran has one of the most unique minds I've ever encountered. She doesn't develop tricks to excel in competition. Instead, she focuses on the near impossible. I first met her in 2017 after the World Yoyo Contest in Iceland. After the contest, a bunch of people stopped over in London, England and had a meetup in a park.

Rain sprinkled down on us on and off, pushing us under the cover of a large tree. It was here that I spotted Luna sitting on a branch about 6 feet off the ground. Her shoes were on the grass below her, and unlike the rest of us, she didn't have a yoyo in hand. Instead she had the string tied to one foot and was whipping the string around the other foot as the yoyo landed a complex formation. It's a trick called a "Brent Stole" that after 10 years of yoyoing I still can't do with my *hands*.

Later that day, Luna introduced me to "Full Loop," a style she pioneered. You take the string and tie the ends together in an unbroken loop so you are playing with the yoyo spinning detached from the string. She's developed the Full Loop style to a competitive level—and this is just the tip of the iceberg. She hunts out new ways to yoyo, including techniques that would never occur to me. I asked her why she spends her yoyoing time so far outside the box. She explains:

> *The satisfaction of learning and landing a new trick is one of the best feelings I know in the world. Something that calls out to me is trying different styles that are uncommon. Recently, I've been working with a style called Full Loop, which I've never seen performed before. Developing fundamentals from scratch is a challenging process but seeing the reactions from other yoyoers when they see it makes all the work worth it. The new opening into entirely different possibilities lets me explore the furthest reaches of my imagination. Personally, whenever I see someone developing a new style, it's like discovering yoyoing all over again.*

Her words sum it up perfectly. Most yoyoers occasionally dabble in different styles. When I met Luna, I had hit a creative slump with yoyo. When I picked up Full Loop, it was like starting yoyo all over again! It drove me back into playing and creating new tricks.

Zammy

One of the more well known innovators goes by the name Zammy. He was the official "Trick Innovator of the Year" in 2012 for his work developing the style "Möbius." This style involves taking the loop you usually put your finger in, stretching it out, and using it as part of the yoyo trick. It adds such a layer of difficulty (let go at the wrong time and you'll have a tangled mess) that few players take up the challenge. I've tried a few times but didn't get very far. I asked Zammy to share how he got into the style and how he develops his tricks.

> *Back in the early 2000s, I watched a World Yoyo Contest video in which Doc Pop was doing his famous 'Hoopla' trick. I remember*

learning it and loving the style, but technology at the time wasn't what up to what I wanted to do. I let it be and played 1a instead.

At the 2005 Wisconsin State Yoyo Contest held in Madison, WI. I met a fellow known as Alex Berenguel. He showed me the rules and guidelines of Möbius, and I took it and ran with it. There are no real set-in-stone rules for Möbius, but I have tried to create a guideline via my tutorials and tricks. 'R' hold and the 'L' hold describe where the knot part of the loop points, to the direction of right or left. Each hold specializes in certain tricks.

Development happens via constant experimentation. Lots of 'trick paths.' I take, edit, mutate, and decide if I want to go further. Kind of like when an artist is painting a picture, she/he has a vision and has to go with the flow. For me it's like painting mixed with critical thinking and experimentation.

Zammy continues to push the boundaries with Mobius, and like so many other yoyoers, uses it to connect with the community.

While Zammy and Luna work on developing styles that few others play, Steve Brown and Jon Gates are yoyoers who have taken a common style one step further. They both developed yoyo trick styles that went on to become official competition divisions. In both cases, it was a lot of hard work combined with the right timing.

Steve Brown - The Invention of 5a

The style we now call "5a" or "Freehand" is a standard competition style. Nearly every yoyoer dabbles at some point by tying a die, a ball, or some other small object to the end of a string. I once had a student poke a hole in an eraser and use that! Yet 5a hasn't always been a mainstay of yoyo.

Steve tells his story:

It was 1998, and I had been hanging out a lot with Mark McBride. These kids were doing 'Slippery Eel' tricks. They were playing with a Yomega Raider, a responsive yoyo. They would take the finger loop off their finger, swing the yoyo under the leg and catch the string on the other side. I was having an awful time. It made yoyo bigger and more like juggling, something I wanted to do but I couldn't achieve. The finger loop knot was too tiny to catch. I chatted with Mark McBride, and he handed me a tiny plastic bead. 'Thread the string through this thing, then you can feel when you reach the end.' I tried that without success because it whipped by my hand too fast.

Sometime later I was in Chino, California with a couple of the Team Losi guys. I told them about this problem. One of them gave me a few cancelled casino dice with holes in them and said, 'Try this.' He kept a bunch on a long wallet chain. I threw them in my pocket and promptly forgot about them.

Three weeks later, while doing laundry, I found the dice and gave it a shot. I strung one onto the end of the string and threw a trapeze. My allergies had been acting up, and as soon as I hit the trapeze, I sneezed! I dropped the die and it swung over into my other hand perfectly. I kind of looked at the yoyo and swung it up and repeated the motion with the other hand.

First thing I did? Left-handed everything! I remembered an old Duncan demonstrator who could do all the contest tricks with both hands. Immediately I thought 'This will be awesome! I'm going to be the guy who is 100% ambidextrous!' The most useless thing imaginable for yoyo in the days before 3a, but I was excited!

I kept fiddling around. I found points in the middle of tricks where I could drop the die and make something happen. I tried Double or Nothing, Brain Twister, anything I could manage. All the original ideas were 'Do an existing trick, drop the weight, then practice!'

This built up to the 1999 BAC (Bay Area Classic) routine, which is the first time I showed 5a to anybody. And when I did it...nobody cared. The next year, once again, nobody cared. For the first two or three years Chris Neff (another Duncan demonstrator) and I were the only people playing with a die.

We experimented with what we called "Wallys" where we hurled the yoyo at walls, shot the yoyo up skate ramps, and threw it *against anything else we could think of. Everything was new, being hyper creative was easy because there wasn't anything else to compare. Literally every time I picked the yoyo up, I created a trick.*

Over time other players picked it up, so I looked into getting a patent. It costs $18,000, and I had $400 in my checking account. So, I made a deal with Duncan. They covered the costs and got control of the patent. In exchange, they paid me a royalty. I ended up with 1.5%, which is horrible. In retrospect, this was likely the stupidest business choice I've ever done, and that's saying a lot.

I would have been better off finding another way to pay for that patent. I could have licensed it out to everybody at a more affordable rate and more brands would be selling 5a yoyos. I would have earned significantly more money. Instead I gave the rights to a company that never really understood what 5a meant to the yoyo community. They never did much of anything with it. Probably the biggest disappointment of my entire career.

The good news is that the patent runs out in 2020. Then everyone can make 5a yoyos. It's a style that hasn't grown as much as it could, possibly because no brands other than Duncan are able to promote it (without paying a fee to Duncan). If you want to keep track of how long until the trademark is up, head over to 5ayoyo. com."

Usually, when someone sneezes, the only thing they pass along to others is a cold. Steve passed along a whole new world of yoyo tricks! Anthony Rojas talked about limitations on innovation. I think the biggest difference between 1998 and 2020 is organization. Yoyo has grown and now has rules and structures, institutions and scheduled events. Innovation doesn't have the viral potential it used to when big brands had the spending power to push a new style out into the world. Change happens more slowly and in smaller groups. Perhaps one day, new styles of play will join the big five at contests. For now, the folks sneezing their way into new styles have one benefit that Steve lacked—access to the internet.

Jon Gates - The 4a "Bind"

One of Steve Brown's contemporaries, Jon Gates, had a similar experience to Steve's. His moment of innovation started a new style and, in some ways, opened the door to modern yoyoing.

Modern yoyo tricks require an "unresponsive" yoyo—one that doesn't return on a tug. Instead, you need to use a trick called a "bind" to bring the yoyo back. Jon stumbled on this trick back when an "unresponsive" yoyo was a broken yoyo.

My preferred competition division is "Offstring" or "4a." Jon's contribution is a key component of this style. He spent years as a professional yoyoer during the 1990s, travelling and demonstrating. For years before Jon, yoyoers messed around with detaching the yoyo from the string and throwing it like a spin top. This was a novelty, a trick to amaze the crowd. When the yoyo stopped spinning, however, it had to be wound up again. It wouldn't return to the hand. It was Jon who figured out how to get the yoyo to return, opening the door to a whole new style of yoyoing!

Today Jon spends his days making wooden yoyos. Some have fixed wooden axles, others ball bearings. John hand turns them with care and precision in his workshop. He showed me one design he's working on that looks like a solid body design but is in fact hollow. He works with a range of wood types with many designs.

I asked Jon to share the fabled story of how he invented the offstring "bind" trick.

> I started yoyoing in 1988. I picked my first one up in 1976. But it wasn't until I was a junior in high school that I got hooked as did most kids. Kids that age have no idea what they want to do with their lives. I thought I'd be a pro skateboarder. That dream didn't pan out, but I managed to get pretty good at yoyo.

> When I graduated there were two big events for yoyoing going on. Yoyo was part of the international juggling festival. We did big yoyo workshops and got jugglers into playing yoyoing. The event was a teaching program that Dale Oliver pulled together for the brand Playmax.

> I got there and found disappointment. I already knew almost all the tricks they were teaching; I was 18 years old. I was very

inventive; I was making up variations of tricks and in some ways this frustrated Dale Oliver. He wanted to show me a few tricks and make me go practice while he worked with others!

He was like, 'All right. I've got one that'll distract you,' and he took the yoyo off the string and wound it up. I said 'Yeah, I know this trick, it's the Runaway Dog.' He says, 'No check this out.' Then did a very unusual throw. Palm to the ground, he pushed it straight down, then pulled up at the last second. The same way you throw a spin top, catching it on the string. I asked him to do it again and he couldn't repeat it. He looked at me and said, 'Good enough, go work on it.'

Well I went nuts trying to figure this out. I stayed up till something like three in the morning playing trying to figure out how to make this thing work.

At that point I had played Diabolo a little and could do a few tricks. One Diablo trick called 'The Elevator' involved wrapping the string around it and pulling so it climbs up the string. I tried that with the offstring yoyo. To my surprise, the yoyo pulled the tip of the string out of my left hand and shot right up into my right hand!

I threw it again, caught it on the string, [and it] went back to my hand the second time and then a chill came over me. I felt goose bumps all over my arms, and it was like, 'Wait a minute, I've figured something out.'

A third throw and again, the yoyo returned to my hand. I was by myself in this hotel room, jumping up and down and grinning like a madman. I figured out something I don't think anybody else had ever figured out.

The next day I went back to the conference area. Bob Maloney and Dennis McBride were there with Dale. I asked Dale 'When you do that trick when the yoyo is disconnected, how do you get the yoyo to return to your hand?'

I though he'd figured this out already. He looked at me like I was joking. He said 'It's not connected. It's like a spinning top. You throw it and it spins and then the trick's over.'

So I threw it, caught it and did the trick to wind it back before I looked at him again. I threw it again and did a Brain Twister Somersault and I wound it back. I looked up at him and I remember the look on his face as well as Dennis and Bob's. All three of them were standing there with their mouths open.

I learned later that some older demonstrators used flying yoyo tricks (without the yoyo returning to the hand) as a way to promote the 'Butterfly' yoyo. It was a great marketing trick, because kids would try it, break their yoyo, then need to buy a new one!

What a fantastic origin story for the style! I asked Jon to share what happened next, and how "Offstring" became a standard division in yoyo. He explains:

Later, I was touring with Team High Performance and Alan Nagao saw me doing 'flying yoyo' tricks. He invited me to be the head of a new promotional project, 'Team Hyper Viper.' The idea was to promote offstring yoyo (he gave it the name that stuck). It was a fun time, I met up with John Higby every week and we'd trade offstring tricks, pushing each other to get better.

At one point we were in Japan performing. They told us 'Get up on stage and do your hardest tricks!' What we didn't know was that the MC was telling the audience that these were all easy beginner tricks. This meant that the kids watching started practicing these tricks, thinking they were easy. And it worked! They were amazing and challenged the USA players to get even better, it made a great feedback loop of skill development.

Jon has had a fascinating career in the yoyo world. What a great contribution! I love the last bit of that story. In my almost decade and a half teaching elementary school, I've learned one thing for certain. Never tell a kid what they can't do. If you show them something hard, then tell them it's easy, they'll take up the challenge and blow you away.

Inspiration comes from the strangest places. "Where do you get your ideas?" is a question that frustrates artists the world over. My personal response is, "How do YOU make the ideas stop? They drive me crazy!" That said, the innovators in this section think so far beyond me that I can't begin to understand where they get their ideas. Artists don't have more ideas than everyone else; they have simply trained themselves to notice when they have an idea and act on it. Yoyo is an art form, and when you spend enough time doing something, ideas will come.

No one invents anything in a vacuum. When Steve Brown invented 5a, he didn't create a brand new thing out of nowhere. I've seen pictures of a yoyo that came with an attached counterweight, sold well before Steve's discovery. Similarly, Jon didn't invent 4a, as others were already detaching the yoyo from the string before he came up with the "bind." Both players took building blocks from others who came before them and re-arranged them in a way that caught on and became part of the culture. Innovation is collaborative, as human brains work better together.

Chapter 17: Family of Yoyoers

Yoyoing is a weird thing to do. It's a sport with a long history and worldwide recognition, but it's not something you see every day. Yoyoers can be obsessed, but we get away with it because of the support of family and friends. For the younger players, parents are the real heroes. It's a standard thing for MCs at contests to thank the organizers, the sponsors, and above all, the parents and families that brought us all together.

My wife is my hero. She doesn't just tolerate my yoyoing; she revels in it. I find myself performing for strangers because Mrs. Yoyothrower grabs my arm and says, "Look at this cool thing my husband can do!" Our vacation plans revolve around contests more often than not—although my wife didn't complain about the three-week honeymoon in Italy that came along with our trip to the World Yoyo Contest in Prague. My best friend even helped me write this book, which is a testament to a friendship. Below are some thoughts shared by the family and friends of yoyoers.

Josh Prokay passed along his fiancée **Alicia's** thoughts on his hobby:

Alicia always said she thought it was cool. She didn't seem thrilled to go to her first contest, but we ended [up] befriending many new people and she had a great time. She couldn't wait for the next one. She's been getting into yoyos recently, but thinks it can be a bit frustrating.

Takaki Clark's **mother** shares her thoughts on his yoyo career:

After he started to compete, he had more variety of friends from all over the world. And as long as he enjoys yoyo, he can keep working towards his achievement. But it is noisy all over the house when he is practicing.

I suspect most family members share her opinion when it comes to the noise. I've heard numerous parents complain about it over the years. My response is generally to list the many, many things kids can do that are a lot more irritating. "I could have handed them a harmonica" generally works.

Abby Brodsky reflects on the mixed reviews she gets from her siblings:

They say it's annoying having your sister yoyo in front of the TV. The sound of a yoyo bearing spinning gets old quickly. My siblings love talking about the times I have hit my face with a yoyo. I've received a few gashes from getting clocked in the head.

Andre Hurtado asked his **best friend** to share their opinion of the hobby.

Andre always shows an excessive amount of hype anytime he watches either a Betty, Keiran, Sean, Javier, Iori, or Takeshi freestyle. You can just see the sheer happiness and excitement in his eyes.

Jordan Bowlan (soon to be Jordan Blair) seems to share my wife's fascination when it comes to what her partner does with a yoyo. She says:

My future husband is an avid yoyo fiend and creator! Honestly, one of my favorite things is when I introduce him to someone new, or even someone he has met before. He tells them about what he does for a living. Often, I hear people say something like, 'What? Yoyos? Do kids even play with those anymore?' I love the look on their faces when he shows them videos of championships, but the greatest thing of all is when he busts out his own yoyo and throws it.

People are absolutely blown away by what he can do with a yoyo in his hands. They go from, 'Is there really that big of a market for yoyos?' to gathering a crowd of friends saying, 'You have to see what this guy can do!' I could honestly sit around and watch him yoyo for hours at a time just to keep myself entertained. That is until I get frustrated that he is immensely cooler than I am.

Ash Brooks loves how yoyo is a part of her husband's life. She shares:

My husband, Bradford, is a yoyoer and dragged me into this cool little world! He has always had an interest, but only recently has he been able to buy yoyos and practice and learn new tricks. The main thing that I have come to enjoy with his hobby is watching my kids smile, giggle, and be amazed while he does even the most basic of throws. It has become something my four-year-old daughter wants to learn, and my one-year-old loves to watch.

We bought my four-year-old a Duncan Butterfly, she can get it down just not back up. Our one-year-old has a Dollar Tree yoyo. He loved to drag it around and 'play' with it. I am a crafter as my hobby, and it is something easy for kids to join in on. Most of my husband's other hobbies are not good for kids, but this has given them a way to connect.

I am not really interested in throwing, but I have tried and want to learn the basics. I have made a few things for his collection, which seems never ending, and keep trying to create new things.

Playing together is good for family bonds. As kids, we learn empathy and social skills through play. As adults, we bond through shared hobbies and time spent being ridiculous. One of the great struggles in the developed world right now is maintaining a feeling of connectedness. Yoyo seems to provide that.

Audrey is the partner of a yoyoer (Yeti B.), and she has also found a place in the yoyo world. It has been a privilege to be a part of her journey. She shares:

All my life I have struggled with social anxiety, especially in big crowds. The room goes black, I get dizzy, and claustrophobia kicks in. When I first met Yeti, he made the community seem so amazing and I knew I wanted to be part of it. But I was also aware it meant I had to get out of my comfort zone.

Then, I was fortunate enough to meet Ray from MonkeyFingeR. He thinks I'm doing him a favor by selling his products at competitions, but it goes both ways. By representing his products, I get to be part of the action, meet tons of people, and it keeps me busy while Yeti meets his millions of fans (joking). Plus, being behind the table helps make me feel safe and less anxious.

One of the best parts was the time a yoyo promo video turned into a wedding proposal. So many yoyoers came together for this. MonkeyFingeR Ray made a special yoyo and ghosted 'WILL YOU MARRY ME' on it. Coffin, from OhYesYo, made a personalized ring box and Dukes, Becci, Mr. Yoyothrower & Diamond filmed everything and made my day wonderful.

How I feel about being the partner of a yoyoer depends on the day. Some days it's fun and I really get into it. I want to jump in the deep end, start a yoyo team, maybe even start yoyoing and become a champion. But other days, it is expensive and/or time consuming. Overall though, the community has been so amazing and makes my hairy beast happy, so I'm happy!

I spotted an Instagram post by **Denise** and (with permission) had to include it:

I often get asked if I ever tire of watching my husband perform. And I always say never, it's always new. The priceless reaction of the audience and their jaws dropping just make me so proud and honored to be there supporting him. Like, 'Wow, a yoyo can do that!? HE can do that!'

Having a partner that takes joy in your pursuit of a passion is an amazing thing.

We are a strange bunch, but no different from your average hockey fan. People like to share interests and hobbies with a group, and for many of us, that group is yoyoers. There may be a laundry list of different ways to enjoy the hobby, but we all love the same thing—that simple spinning toy.

Chapter 18: Aging in the Yoyo Community

I began yoyoing in my late twenties. I felt a little awkward competing against kids 10-15 years younger than me. Now, at almost 40, I feel positively ancient sitting amongst the majority of players. The technical skill of younger yoyoers on Instagram makes it easy to say, "Why bother, I'll never get there."

Veteran competitor and world level judge **Dennis Shatter's** experience highlights this:

> I started competing when I was 12 years old.
> I gave up when I was 18.

There is no question that the yoyo scene is bottom heavy when it comes to age. New kids discover yoyo, dive in, and then drift towards other hobbies. Those who stuck with the hobby into adulthood, rediscovered it as adults, or started as adults are all a little different. Don't get me wrong. The younger yoyoers are the lifeblood of the sport. A lot of the innovation and drive comes from them.

Physically demanding competitive sports will always be the domain of the young. Yoyo is no different. The time required isn't available to most older adults (due to family, work, and other hobbies). The physical toll of hours of repetitive practice is harder to tolerate as you age. There are still plenty of adults competing, but few make it anywhere near the top. Most world champions are in their late teens and early twenties.

There exists a space for older yoyoers at the World Yoyo Contest. I foresee an explosion of talent in the "Over-40" division in the next few years. Many players who were champions in the early 2000s will qualify. I am looking forward to being able to relax and throw at a speed that doesn't risk breaking a hip or giving me a heart attack! (That's right, you kids there... get off my lawn!)

Does a yoyo player's skill fade with age? Can a player who starts in their twenties or thirties still compete? Some argue that while skill itself doesn't wane, coordination, muscle ability, and stamina do. The ability to remember tricks can fade. The biggest issue is time. As we age, responsibilities devour our yoyoing time. A pesky job, the deluge of bills and those needy children! I mean, come on, do you need to eat more than once a day? Laundry? Just wear the same pants five days in a row, no one will notice!

As you explore the yoyo world, you find sub-communities. Some people like to share their love for spicy foods and yoyos. Others just want to have adult conversations. You know, things like, "Gah, my mortgage payments are crazy right now." A Facebook group called "Drink Beer and Yoyo" comprises people posting photos of their throw and their beverage of choice for that day.

While the older generation may have less free time, they also have the experience and problem-solving ability to make connections and target their limited practice time in a way a 12-year-old can't. Still, that only takes you so far.

I asked **Greg Pettit** if aging has had an impact on his yoyo skills. He says:

I think it must [have]. I have never been great shakes at yoyo, but my muscles, eyesight, memory—none of it helps when I'm trying to get those nutty speed combos down. With enough practice, I can master the weird and interesting tricks, but not fast competition stuff. I'm also aware of aging when I train [at] Muay Thai Kickboxing. I remember what it was like to react quickly to stimulus (slipping a punch coming at you and countering with your own strike). My mind remembers the feeling, but my body doesn't have the ability to respond as fast anymore.

My body is starting to betray me. But I still have plenty of fun (at both yoyo AND kickboxing)!

Every time I hit the basketball court, I feel what Greg is talking about. I play in a co-ed league that's pretty chill, but I play with folks as young as 20. There's an element of speed I can't match. I can't jump as high or move as fast. I have to rely on "old man smarts" and outthink them, using better team play and communication and studying the court to predict what will happen next. That's not an option in yoyo. It's all about muscle memory and speed.

Nathan Loding, on the other hand, doesn't buy age as a barrier. He says:

I think you need to define 'successful.' Can you do some amazing combos and tricks and have a blast doing it? Absolutely. Will you be a world champion? That'll be hard, but I'd argue it would be due more to the time commitment than age.

One of my favorite lines from my father-in-law (Bob Norton) is "It's tough getting old, but it beats the alternative." He's the happiest man in the nursing home, spending his days socializing and taking part in every program available. Bob has the right idea. While I'm still counting on nanotechnological immortality coming through in my lifetime, I'll do my best to maintain a positive attitude towards aging. Yoyo is a great way to keep my mind working and my dexterity up. As long as I'm careful not to overdo it, I'll still be carrying around a yoyo in my nineties!

Part 3

Bringing the Edges Together

Finding Balance In Yoyo

UP AND DOWN THE STRING
FOCUS AND MEDITATION
SOMETIMES HIT YOUR HEAD

It takes the outliers of society and it gives them a common bond. The yoyo industry and the community bring these people together. It's for everyone.

— Chris Allen

This chapter is the reason I started writing this book. I've crossed paths with more diverse people in yoyo than in any other hobby. As a whole, yoyoers don't fit into any particular "category" in society. They aren't divided by race, religion, nationality, job, money, class, or politics. Chance, timing, and a bit of destiny bring us together. So many of us have hit troubled waters in life, and this old-fashioned toy is like a lighthouse in a storm.

When talking to yoyoers, the common thread seems to be finding a missing sense of belonging. People have a need for something to bring calm and focus, something to help manage their daily struggle in one way or another. Yoyo can be a powerful tool to manage thoughts, feelings, or a body that betrays us in everyday life—the challenges that keep us from being "normal" and fitting in. In yoyo, we've found a home, a place where we can be weird, stand proud, and feel included in a group—individual, but important in our own way. Yoyo brings the edges together to make a stronger whole.

Failure is a valuable life skill. If you talk to anyone at the top of their field, they will have stories of times they crashed and burned. The thing that ties them together is that they got up, dusted themselves off, and did what was necessary to move on. Yoyo is one of the greatest teachers of this skill. You cannot have any kind of success with a yoyo unless you are willing to dedicate yourself to overcoming constant failure. The act of learning the basic throw takes hundreds of attempts to get right.

In this final section, I want to talk about surviving hardship and finding joy in yoyo. I'll briefly share my story and then dive into stories from various members of the yoyo community.

Chapter 19: My Journey

My upbringing wasn't picture-perfect, but it was pretty good. Mom and I lived in my grandparent's basement suite in a suburb of Vancouver until I was seven, when she remarried. I grew up surrounded by love. Mom has seven siblings and I've over 30 first cousins. Much of my childhood as spent at various aunts' and uncles' places or running around the neighborhood catching critters in the creek and playing in the forest.

Mom worked nights, and she often woke up Sunday mornings with me next door at my friend Ryan's house having pancakes. I had the freedom to grow and experience challenges.

Dad works hard and tries to take care of everyone around him. His number one goal is for people he loves to find happiness, whatever that looks like. Mom is a hippie in the best sense of the word. A school principal who spends her days showing everyone they are loved and cared about. When I teach, I try to be like her and remember that everyone needs to feel valued and loved if they are to find success.

Clumsiness has colored my entire life. I'm also an emotionally sensitive person. I take things seriously, and when I hurt, I hurt hard. My first nickname was "Wimpy Willers" (Willers was my childhood last name). I'm not a fighter, and it baffled me that there weren't more rational ways to solve disputes.

As a kid I got hurt a lot. I had a disorder as a child that meant my muscles didn't develop in sync with one another. Most of the time I couldn't walk 10 steps without tripping over myself. Many, many trips to the hospital for tests finally brought the vague diagnosis of "Non-degenerative Muscular Dystrophy." The treatment? "He'll likely grow out of it."

I was bullied because I was different, clumsy, wouldn't fight back, and sometimes just because I was there.

I got through it thanks to supportive family and good friends. I grew eight inches taller during my Grade 6 year, and found my first grand passion in life: basketball. My nickname was "Lurch" in high school. The running joke was that I tripped over the lines on the basketball court.

I persevered through many, many hours a day of practice, beyond what the other players needed. Forcing my muscles to work together, earning the respect of my peers, and a starting position on the team. An incredible sense of community helped me through those troubling teenage years.

As an adult, I live with a painful nervous system disorder due to car accidents. The yoyo community has sustained me through adjusting to more limited activities. While there are many things I can't do anymore, I strive to find new hobbies and new ways of doing things. Having a yoyo business gives me the excitement and joy I used to find through competition.

I live with ADHD. I don't idle well. I have a hard time waiting and forget basic things. This isn't being forgetful in the sense of "Oh, I have a terrible memory." It's the complete inability to recall the name of someone I've known for a decade. It's hard for people to understand being cognitively incapable of remembering things on demand.

I can't attach faces to names without substantial effort and a lot of time. If an object isn't right in front of me, it ceases to exist. Things stored in drawers or cupboards are gone forever.

Twice, the kind attendant from the gas station across the street returned my dog when I walked her over there after a long workday, tied her outside, and then stumbled home without her. It broke my heart each time when I thought about how scared and confused she must have been.

Routine is my best friend. Everything stays in my pockets at day's end. In the morning, everything is transferred from yesterday's pants to today's.

The hardest part to cope with is the skewed sense of time. An ADHD brain processes time differently. For me there is: "now" and "not-now." If you tell me to do something right now, I'm on it. If it has to be done in 20 minutes, it's not going to happen. I rely on timers, calendar notifications, and my wife to keep me from getting lost in whatever I'm doing.

Being introverted and fidgety isn't great for large social settings. In fact, I took up the guitar so I would have something to do at parties. I got through university on sheer determination, learning to accept that I would never be more than a B student. I couldn't focus to study, couldn't memorize facts, and struggled to get major projects finished. "The best is the enemy of good enough" is how I live my life.

My calling was to be a teacher—a job less about the details and more about the big picture. I can bring joy, showing support and understanding for the kids in my classes. I can relate to kids who are constantly angry and upset because nobody gets them. I hope the kids who struggle with ADHD or don't fit in get a year of reprieve with me, a year with a teacher who has been in their shoes and knows what it's like. Teaching led me to yoyo.

When the NED show came to my school, I had no clue my life was about to change. The kids bought yoyos, I did too, and a page turned in my life. It was something to keep my hands busy, and the reward of learning a trick came fast so I stuck with it.

I have taught many kids to yoyo throughout the years. Many were what we call in teaching "grey area" kids—the ones who stand out not because of learning challenges or academic exceptionalities. Not obvious outcasts or picked on kids, but ones who didn't click with offered activities and got lost in the shuffle.

I taught yoyo during lunch time and recess, and these kids flourished. I saw the beginning of patterns which have repeated throughout my career. A kid living with autism had a place to connect and communicate. One with ADHD found joy being part of something. A shy kid took it very, very seriously, coming out of their shell a bit, while an outgoing child would help teach others. After yoyo club has been introduced at school, teachers and parents report:

> My child was impossible," they might say. "They wouldn't stick with anything, never demonstrated the ability to learn a skill. Now they are focusing and driven, sticking with something for the first time in their life.

There are common threads when people explain why they yoyo:

> "Yoyo has helped with my ADHD."

"It gives me time away from my computer."

"Throwing helps me calm my mind when I'm feeling stress or anxiety."

There may be a medical text to be written on the physical and mental benefits of yoyo. Perhaps doctors should be prescribing yoyo as therapy! I know I'd be happy if my extended medical coverage paid for my strings.

There are few things in life more valuable than the ability to step away from stress for a moment and talk about something unrelated to your daily grind. Yoyo provides that outlet.

Chapter 20: The Strings that Bind Us

THE STRINGS THAT BIND US,
THE HANDS THAT WIND US
THE STEEL INSIDE US
ADD UP TO ONE THING:
WHEN LEARNING, BE DARING
DON'T LOSE YOUR BEARINGS,
FOR OTHERS KEEP CARING
AND ALWAYS PICK UP YOUR STRING.

Some of the following stories warrant a trigger warning, as some yoyoers discuss dark moments in their lives around self-harm and addiction and how yoyo has helped them get through. You'll see three asterisk's beside the names for those stories.

Chris Allen

Chris Allen is a pillar of the yoyo community. He's been less active in recent years, but his work building yoyoskills.com was invaluable to a generation of yoyoers. Chris has brought joy through sharing and teaching yoyo tricks. His story below shows how yoyo weaves together the lives of so many people. You can't label a yoyoer based on who they are or where they come from; we are too different. We share this hobby and that's all the definition we need.

What we do is stress relief. Yoyoing is learning. It is socialization. It is private or performance. It is everything that you can put your power [of] personality behind. It is raw, polite, rude, and an outlet for that personality. If you look around the industry, you'll see all these styles growing. Yoyo is incredible because it takes the outliers of society and gives them a common bond. The yoyo industry and the community bring these people together. Yoyo is for everyone.

Everybody has good and bad days; it's up in the air. A lot of kids come to yoyo club because their parents don't know what to do with them. They are not into sports and they play video games for most of the day. Yoyo forces them to be social when maybe they don't want to. It helps them achieve motor skills and develops those parts of their brain that don't get a lot of exposure because the kids are behind a computer or controller for most of the day.

A lot of kids aren't going to be into basketball, baseball, or football, but they excel in yoyoing. Shy kids who will learn to ask others how to do tricks. Those who have a hard time with authority learn how to approach instructors politely and ask for help. Kids who have ADHD or anxiety issues can take things and break them down into smaller steps or speed things up. That's the magic of yoyoing.

I get excited when I see a kid hold the yoyo the right way and throw it down, turning it in their hands without bouncing and then pulling up and catching it. Their face lights up because they've been trying to manage on their own for weeks. Until that moment, the yoyo always turns sideways, or the spin dies or gets caught in their finger instead of rolling off naturally. But when you're helping them and they figure it out, this light bulb goes off.

From that moment on, they know how to throw. It's unforgettable. You are making a permanent stamp on that child's brain. This is something that they accomplished and will never forget.

Coffin Nachtmahr

Coffin Nachtmahr is many things: artist, skater, performer, yoyoer. A few years ago, an award-winning documentary called *Throw* told his story. He speaks about how yoyo helped him manage the intense challenges of life as a youth in Baltimore. Yoyo helps him lift up the people around him. He and I collaborated on a yoyo (The Sk8r) and had great fun making an art piece out of it.

Yoyoing was lifesaving to me; it offered me opportunity. My friends and I travel because [of it] and we are welcomed in places we never would have been. Yoyo has given me a job and keeps the lights on at home. Most importantly, throwing gives me peace of mind and a sense of community.

I've been loads of places now, I'm in a film that's been seen by loads of people. It brings positive light to the black youth in Baltimore. I've been invited to events within my own city I didn't know existed. When you think of the Emmys, you don't picture people who look like me at all. But throwing took me there.

Luna Harran

Luna Harran has one of the most creative minds I've ever encountered. Yoyo has provided consistency in her life, an anchor through the tough times. It's provided a much-needed community of similar minds who share ideas.

Skill toys give me something to hold on to. It helps me break the ice with people when I first meet them. Something to hide behind when I feel nervous and something I can share with confidence.

The creative community has given me people to talk to, to share ideas with, and a pool of people much bigger than I ever thought I'd be able to reach. When I was going through some harder periods of my life, practicing skills gives me something constant. Somewhere to channel my emotions and turn them into something constructive. A tool to turn to when I need comfort or company.

Yoyoing has always been what I needed to come to grips with the world. I wouldn't trade that for anything.

Ash Brooks (***)

Ash Brooks is married to a yoyoer (Bradford Brooks) and values the connection and support it provides for him.

Yoyo has given my husband a supportive and loving community. This past year we got the great news that we were expecting our third little monkey. Only a short time later, we got the devastating news that we had lost the baby and suffered a miscarriage.

At the time, both of us were working. It sent both of us into a dark place, and to top it off Brad lost his job. Neither of us were able to support each other as we needed. One day Brad just needed to get his feelings out and made a post on the forums. The love and support that came from this was amazing for him.

Yoyo really helped him get back in a good place. I couldn't be more grateful that they could help support him when I could not. Even though what happened was in NO way related to yoyos, it made me see that this community is more of a family that love and support each other, rather than a group of strangers that like the same thing.

In September (2019) we went to Disney World. Somehow, we made our way to the Duncan yoyo booth twice in Disney Springs. While we were there Brad got to meet three or four local Orlando yoyoers, and I enjoyed watching them bond. They showed each other their throws and showed each other tricks they were working on. It really showed how sweet a community of people can be.

Zammy (***)

Zammy is one of the most interesting and creative members of our community. He's spent his career innovating and pushing the boundaries of what one can do with a yoyo. He struggles emotionally and has relied on the support of the community through a series of personal losses. I had the privilege of meeting him at the 2018 USA National Championships.

> When I arrived at the Palmer House (USA Nationals host hotel) with Nehemiah that Friday night, I walked up the steps and I was so nervous. But when I saw all the people, it was amazing. When I made my appearance, tons of throwers started to throw the Möbius style! I've never seen so many at once. It was as if everyone in the room was playing it and all it took was for me to show up. It was a very emotional feeling, a moment of clarity. When we all got back to the Residence Inn Marriott, I was talking about that key moment and Markmont said to me, 'That's a powerful moment.'

> The most difficult part of the contest was keeping my paranoia, agoraphobia, and social anxiety in check. Look, I'm a country bumpkin. I don't get out much, nor am I a city person. I don't know how to travel on my own, I get lost all the time, I absolutely hate crowds. I specifically spoke with Nehm, Drew, and Will about this to keep an eye on me.

> Going to Chicago was a huge undertaking, since it's such a big city with tons of people everywhere. And being at the contest itself was harsh on me, because of so many people close together. I can be distant until I get close enough to trust someone. My paranoia creeps up and I get a feeling like as if everyone in this community is out to get me/hates me/talks behind my back. That's why I just latch on to certain folk like the Onedrop guys. They respect me and invited me with open arms and understood my emotions when it came to that. They kept me in check. They kept me good.

> I contribute everything that I am to this silly little toy called a 'yoyo.' With that said, I've outright told people it has saved my life because without yoyo, frankly, I wouldn't be here. Unfortunately, I have clinical depression, which often gives me a clouded sense of reality.

Once upon a time, I was a self harmer, with over ninety scars across my left arm. I've almost committed suicide too. But thanks to yoyoing, I could turn my frustrations with myself and the world and bring about a positive change. Some days are better than others, but most of the time I'm throwing to calm myself down and tune out the world.

Yoyoing has given me a purpose to keep going in life, because the possibilities in the sub-culture are infinite. There are so many callings ready to be fulfilled, people to meet and share stories with, and friends to make. People I can share smiles with and make memories with at contests or a local club. I often feel a sense of emptiness, but throwers remind me why I am needed and wanted and to keep pushing forward.

Yoyoing reminds me that life can be a wondrous thing.

Anonymous (***)

This player is a top-ranked yoyo competitor who has asked to remain Anonymous. Humans thrive on adversity and challenge. In troubled times, they put their energy into excelling at yoyo.

When I started to play yoyo, it was just a toy. I didn't spend much time with it at first, but then I began to learn tricks. My first trip to the EYYC (European Yoyo Championship) gave me so much determination to improve myself. It became a new lifestyle for me.

In 2016, my dad had a heart attack when I was with him. He recovered, but since that moment, I changed. I had post-traumatic stress disorder. I worried it might happen again, and I wasn't able to sleep. I've had depression and tried to commit suicide. In 2017, I spent five months in hospital and had psychotherapy. I had the yoyo next to me. It helped and still helps me survive. When I feel anxious, I play. Yoyo became more than a lifestyle, it's my emergency brake.

Josh Prokay

Yoyo can be meditation. Time spent concentrated on a single point of focus calms the body and mind. Josh Prokay found yoyo, and with it, he found focus and peace when he needed it the most.

> Yoyo has helped me through many tough times. I first got into yoyos during my freshman year of high school in 2008. I had a very unstable home life, and I was a loner in school. I was diagnosed with depression, general anxiety, and ADHD at age 13. Spending hours a day trying to learn new tricks was a fantastic outlet for my frustrations. An easy escape from my wild thoughts. At 18, I was successfully taken off of all my medications.
>
> Ten years later, yoyos still help me cope with stressors including my job, relationship, and social events. It's so easy to set the phone down, pick up a yoyo, and ignore the world for a few minutes and throw. It can be one of the few things that bring me happiness and a sense of satisfaction. If it weren't for yoyos and the friends I've met because of them my life would have taken a different path. Take it as you want but having a hobby like this can enrich your life in many ways. I'm thankful for that.

Yeti B. (***)

Yeti B's life has been one of hardship and growth, with yoyo woven hrough it. The challenges of living in a small town differ from a big city. connected with Yeti after acquiring a large collection of yoyos from he widow of a yoyoer. Boxes of old pro-yos from when he'd been a demonstrator went to kids, but there were some real gems in there. When was trying to find homes for the more collectible ones, Yeti contacted me, nd I ended up gifting him a bunch to replace some of his stolen collection. I idn't know Bob, but his wife wanted the yoyos to go to good homes. I know he ones that found their way to Yeti are exactly where they should be.

> I lost my dad to cancer when I was 12. We moved to a tiny town called Kirkland Lake from Toronto. I struggled with the loss and fell into the small-town youth issues. Smoking, drugs, and drinking became part of my day to day. My mom did her best to keep me straight, but she missed stuff as I got good at hiding. At

18, my Mom bought me a Coca-Cola yoyo that could 'sleep.' She did this as a lark, trying to get me to quit smoking with a distraction. Little did she know what this would do for me and my life. I was amazed. It spun forever (well for 1998).

I discovered there was a big following with yoyos. A few local stores sold Yomegas, and I purchased a few with the transaxle. The yoyo didn't leave my hand after that. I was smoking back then and at one point, I found myself grabbing a yoyo before the smokes. My brain released the same endorphins and relaxed me. I have not had a cigarette in 20 years now.

I have since lost my mom to cancer. She bought me a lot of my first yoyos, and some were stolen. I did recover many of them, but the wood ones were destroyed as they were left in the snow. I recovered the green (Duncan) Freehand One. It was the last throw she gave me. It is a rare color and is definitely never leaving me again. Depression and anxiety color my life, centered on not being good enough and not being able to finish anything I start. The yoyo has always been there and been something I was good at. Not amazing, but good enough to be a respectable player.

As the great Coffin Nachtmahr says, the yoyo is my security blanket. It's been there for me through everything. I've put it down now and then, but I always go back. Yoyos saved my life. I will say that; without them I would have taken a very different path in life and it not a good one. Now with yoyo in hand, I feel I can do anything.

I am a sponsored player and working on becoming a Judge. I want people to find our little community. They take you in and help. I see it over and over again. There are people to talk to and I turn to them a lot. I still have dark days, but [it helps] to know others who suffer the same as I do and want to listen. I try to help (and often do) but just being there for each other is important. When my team gets more excited than I do, when I slowly land a trick I've been trying for months, it's like I am on top of the world.

James Pendall (***)

For James Pendall, yoyo was a literal lifesaver. Like so many others, the community he found was exactly the one he needed during hard times.

Yoyo is a lifesaver. If I hadn't found my way back into the yoyo community, I'd have sought to commit suicide again. Despite being a husband/father and having my musical aspirations. Not that I place my family or any other activities above or below. But this has truly given a re-affirmed sense of purpose.

I collect with the eyes of a child. I have a greater sense of esteem and enjoy the ability to learn and to create. For someone as introverted as myself, it's helped me to re-establish the social frame of things. Even…being some preoccupation to pacify myself, it's filled a void that had been growing within my adult life.

It's aided me in feeling motivated and having a sense of youth again. I love to self teach, to learn, to be challenged. It's so much more than just a leisure hobby or toy.

Ian Smith

Ian Smith specializes in the two styles that are the most time consuming and, in my opinion, the most difficult to learn. In 4a, you spend your first weeks chasing a yoyo around the room or backyard before you even start learning your first trick. With 3a, you spend untold hours untangling and rewinding two throws—and that's after you teach yourself to use your non-dominant hand. Ian has mastered both at the competition level. I shared a coffee with him at the 2018 USA Nationals and enjoyed getting to know him. We laughed when finding out that we both started yoyoing after the NED show visited our schools!

My name is Ian Smith, and I have been yoyoing for 15 years, ever since I saw the NED show when I was in third grade. I have high-functioning autism and one of my gifts is being able to focus. When something catches my interest, I stay focused and yoyos really caught my interest. The community is super supportive, it's easy to make friends and I always feel included.

Takaki Clark

At age 7, I was diagnosed with autism. I had a hard time in school, and I often struggle in some courses. I got into yoyoing at age 10 when NED yoyos came to Jenny Lind Elementary (where I went to). Both my brother Tomoaki and I picked it up from there, and bought the yoyos at school. A few months after the kids bought the yoyos, most of them quit playing, but my brother and I did not give up.

When I was in Japan in 2010 (a couple months after I started) that is when I found more yoyos and brought them over to the US. After that, my mom discovered Chico Yoyo Club, and that got Tomoaki and I more motivated to learn how to yoyo. When I got there, I learned a lot, made a lot of new friends, and discovered more styles in yoyo.

The first contest I attended was the 2012 US National Yoyo Contest in Chico California, and I was blown away. Before US Nationals 2012, I met the player Ian Smith (who is currently a two time California State 3a champion, and 2018 BAC 4a champion). He introduced me to the style 3a (Thank you to him for helping getting this far in 3a).

In 2014 I started competing in 3a. I was nervous at the time and struggled a lot. I worked a lot more and started improving more and more. I made a lot of new friends in the yoyo scene and helped people who are still learning in yoyo. In 2019 I earned two titles in one year. I still enjoy yoyoing until this day, and I wouldn't have reached this far if I didn't pick one up.

Besides being a yoyo competitor I have many hobbies. I take pictures, I'm a mentor, a teacher at yoyo clubs, and I am focusing on being a trick innovator. The benefit I get from taking pictures is people get to see my work. As a mentor/teacher many people ask me for help, and I am happy to do it. As an innovator I see how people engage with what I am doing. It can be a bit of a challenge because I have a hard time innovating tricks.

The way yoyoing made a significant impact on my life was how it helped me stay focused most of the time. As an autistic individual, it helped me out a lot to remain calm. The trauma I had to go through was losing three of my family members (grandfather, father, then aunt). The only way I can feel better is to yoyo. It helped me cope a lot with anxiety and depression because of my past losses.

Nicholas Vannote

Nicholas Vannote embodies how inward-looking this hobby can be. Those of us who love the spotlight jump on stage any chance we get, but we are the exception. Nicholas is far more the rule. Yoyoers often just want some peace and quiet to develop their skill.

I yoyo purely for its meditative aspects. It helps a lot with my anxiety. While I do it in front of people, it's very personal to me. I hate showing it off to people. It's a very bittersweet, Zen-like activity for me. I lost years to a car accident injury and this community is one of the things that kept me going.

I was born with scoliosis and always had back problems. I had to wear a hard-plastic back brace for 23 hours a day when I was 14. That was to stave off major spinal fusion surgery. I was in that brace for about two years. It did what it was supposed to do, but it was hard.

About 20 years later, my scoliosis had progressed to where surgery was imminent. I had recently injured my back moving a treadmill and my pain steadily got worse. Over the course of the next year, I went from highly functional to bedridden.

On March 1st, 2013, I underwent a five-hour T6 to S1 spinal fusion. Ultimately the fusion did little more than stop my pain from progressing any further. In September 2016, I had a spinal cord stimulator implanted in an attempt to lessen my suffering. The stimulator gave me minor relief.

At that point, I was unable to work or drive. Most of my time was spent in bed. I'm on a cocktail of pain medications and I get regular epidural steroid injections every three months. This regimen keeps my pain at a constant six out of ten on the pain scale.

Fast forward to April 2017. The fidget spinner craze caught me. I read a Reddit post on the fidget spinner forum about the use of yoyo bearings in spinners. I stumbled into r/throwers and read up on modern yoyo play.

I have now been throwing regularly since April of 2017, and it's a hobby that I can do with when I'm out of bed. Throwing is something I can always work on and it doesn't take much time at all. On my high pain days, I can always find a way to throw in between fits and spasms.

My pain meds make concentration and learning a new skill, a major challenge. In the year and a half I've been throwing, I've amassed a nice collection and have enjoyed the support from the yoyo community. For me, throwing is a way for me to cut through the monotony of living with debilitating chronic pain. It's something I can actually do, given my current limitations.

On top of my chronic pain, I also have ADHD, depression, and anxiety problems. Being a part of the yoyo community gives me something to look forward to and something to strive for. There will always be new yoyos to buy and new tricks to learn!

Mike Blake

Many people use special gloves during practice. It would never have occurred to me that wearing yoyo gloves could be a tool that would free someone from social stigma.

I have a laundry list of medical issues and yoyo helps me cope with a lot of them. Moderately severe depression and anxiety color my thoughts. I have severe psoriasis on my hands which is very hard on a yoyo player. First off, because of the psoriasis I wear vinyl gloves 24/7. If I don't, my hands dry up to the point they ball up. If I open them, I will get severe cracks going clear across my palm and it is extremely painful. So, when I yoyo, I wear vinyl gloves and then I wear nylon gloves over top of them. That makes it kind of hard to feel the string. At this point, most of the tricks I do over the last six years of learning are mostly muscle memory.

I used to get stared at because of the gloves. People call me things like "Michael Jackson" or "Danny Glover." I've been dealing with this for a little over 10 years now. In the beginning, it led to my depression and anxiety issues. But yoyoing has helped me overcome the social aspect of the anxiety and a little of the depression.

When I'm throwing, people see somebody who yoyos and has to wear the gloves because of the yoyo, instead of someone who wears gloves all the time. I yoyo on average four to six hours a day because it helps calm me down. It's like a Rubik's Cube with an infinite number of solutions, and there's no right way to do [it].

I have other medical issues too and yoyoing helps me with them. Because it's something I can do that's productive, since there are so many things I can't. My past injuries include breaking my neck, fracturing it twice, and three sprains. Four misplaced ribs and a twisted vertebra in my lower spine add to my difficulties. Osgood-Schlatter's disease limits the use of my knees. And every disc in my neck is a bulging disc.

As you can imagine, it's hard to bend at certain times. But with yoyo, I can be just as good as anybody else. Even if I'm not able to bend and do tricks like behind the back or under the legs.

Joseph Aldrich

I was stuck in the bed for 7 years with a back injury. I had just married the girl of my dreams and was getting started with my career when it happened. Exercise was impossible, standing for more than 10 minutes was agony. By the end my weight crossed the 400lbs mark and depression was a constant. Long story short on the back issue I had been given a second chance at life, but it was a small one.

My recovery had started, and I started to lose about a pound a month. One night while watching videos on YouTube I stumbled on to a video of someone doing some cool tricks with a yoyo. The ADD part of me was hooked. "How can I get in on this and am I capable of doing these cool tricks?"

I started my research and found out there were two kinds of yoyos—responsive and unresponsive. All the advice I was getting told me to start with a responsive yoyo. But the ADHD side of me wanted to jump right in and said 'No, I want the unresponsive yoyo!' So I looked online and bought a cheap Magic Yoyo.

Now I have the yoyo and it's time to start learning these cool awesome tricks. It's funny how many struggle when they throw for the first time. I must have a natural knack for it, as I managed a decent throw the first time. At first the bind took a few days to get right but then I got the hang of it and started to excel. Whenever my wife had to run errands became practice time.

Today I've lost most of my weight with about 80lbs to go. I am in love with this simple thing that has unending possibilities. I will start a job soon for the first time in 7 years. Last night while hanging out with my amazing wife we noticed my right arm looks cut and smaller than my left from yoyoing!

Sampson

Finding this community has honestly changed my life. When I started, I picked up a replay pro, and committed to learning three tricks for my kids. I found that I could not put the gosh-darn thing down, especially in bouts of anxiety, depression, or boredom. It became my form of meditation and a way to ground myself when the world was too much to handle.

I found myself transforming from a short-fused person with borderline personality disorder, into a more grounded and mindful individual. The little joys in life crept back into my world. I stopped caring what others thought and instead placed value on what makes me happy.

Being alive is not the given we believe it to be. That fact should never be overlooked or taken for granted. This enormous epiphany all stemmed from throwing a toy around. Without finding this genuine passion and healthy outlet, I have no idea how I would handle life. I'm so lucky I found this incredible hobby and community.

Yoyo has given me a concrete way of grounding myself. Anytime I feel an 'amygdala attack' coming on, I put my music on, slip on my finger loop, and I'm transported into my own world. A world where nothing matters, and everything is up to me. A place where I can learn new things, work on my flow and transitions, or Eli Hop my way back to happiness. It's a place where I don't have to think, worry, or stress about anything. Instead, I'm focused on myself and my yoyo, working in unison to create something amazing.

Throwing is a form of deep relaxation and expressionism to me. The string is my canvas, the yoyo my brush, and the possibilities are endless.

Bleu Quick

I am a touring/recording musician who is still just starting out. That means I spend a lot of time travelling, living out of a van, going from cheap motel to cheap motel, sometimes living on pennies a week. It can be incredibly rewarding, and it can be intensely stressful. While not all my fellow musicians are accepting of my yoyoing, it does a lot to calm my nerves when I'm home or on the road. I've even met some people who ask if they can try to rip out some Brain Twisters or Rock the Baby! Yoyo means a lot to me as a personal health tool, and to bring me closer to family and friends.

Lauren Palella

If my parents never split up, I would not have started yoyoing. Ok, that seems weird to say but let me explain. It's true. When I was 8, my parents separated. This came as a shock to me because I never saw them fight. They didn't hate each other or anything, they just weren't in love anymore. My mom, brother and I moved to a new town and my dad went to live with his brother. He'd visit every week.

One day he brought over a box with a bunch of stuff he was moving out of his new room that my uncle was throwing out (so my dad could live there). Inside was a yoyo. My dad gave it to me and showed me how to do a forward pass. I got it on the first try though learning to throw properly took another week. I had been doing tricks instead. I entered a talent show a couple months later and after that; I was hooked. Constant learning and a steady stream of yoyos I picked up at the hobby store was my life. I had every old Duncan they had.

I didn't know about contests until I was older. My mom sheltered me from YouTube and the internet in general, [so] I couldn't talk to or meet any other throwers. We couldn't afford to travel to any contests and I'm sure we never would have if we did. Yoyoing was always seen as just a little hobby, but I saw it as much more. I wanted my life to revolve around it. I performed at talent shows, for charities, and a few paid performances.

I broke the mould at 20 when I went to the World Yoyo Contest. My dad and I saved up money to go, and I had the time of my life. I met the people that inspired me to yoyo and work hard in it. I met a lot of awesome people and joined a group on Facebook to become more submersed in the yoyo community. Unfortunately, when I returned home, I had to go back to college. I hated it. I experienced the greatest moment of my life and I had to go to school like it never happened. I graduated with my Associate's [degree] and my next step was my Bachelor's.

By this time, Worlds was back in the US and I knew I was going. I competed again and just like before I got last place. Did I care? No, I wanted to have fun and live my dream again, even if it meant losing. All I ever wanted to do was compete in contests, travel the world, and teach people to throw. Money and time always stopped me, but not anymore. Before I go back to school for my Bachelor's [degree], I plan on traveling to more contests to learn more and be more active.

I struggled a lot in school and didn't have good grades. My only strength was yoyoing, but I struggled to learn or remember my tricks. I practiced every single one every night to remember them. Between struggling in school and things going on in my home life, I was very depressed. My only escape was putting headphones on, blasting music and doing random routines to any song that came up on my MP3 player. I came up with awesome tricks this way but would forget them. I started recording my tricks to remember them on my camera.

I didn't find out about my learning disability until I was already out of high school and into college. From what I learned from my doctor, what I have is usually the result of brain damage. My memory and speech are affected.

My way of fighting this through yoyoing strengthened my ability to remember how to do things. I refuse to let anything hold me back from living my life and doing what I love to do. It's taken me three and a half years to get my Associate's [degree] in Graphic Design, but I won't stop trying until I finish my Bachelor's. And yes, I'm taking my yoyo with me.

For now, I am a collector. I enjoy collecting old school YoYoJam yoyos and other brands I can use to do shows with. I am a teacher. I teach kids and often adults how to yoyo. I am a performer. I perform for charities to help raise money and various shows to inspire others to throw. Yoyoing is my hobby, and hopefully one day I can say it's my entire life.

Dale Oliver

Dale is one of the most influential yo-yoers of our time. He's spent his life surrounded by the joy of teaching children to yoyo and sums up this chapter perfectly.

I have taught over a million children about yoyos in my life. There are hundreds of stories about the positive effects brought about through their involvement. Some of the most dramatic involved ADHD students. Parents thrilled about the change they saw in their children after a short time. The yoyo requires extended attention and hours of practice. It seems that once a child is introduced to this stimulus, the benefits carry over to other areas of their life, including academics.

Many parents are grateful their child gained new confidence and acceptance from their peers through the skills gained with the yoyo.

One story dear to my heart was about four boys the teachers called 'The gang of four.' They told me that on any given day, at least one or more would be in the principal's office. I identified them and recruited them as my assistant teachers. They would give up their recess and lunch play time to come into my yoyo classes to help teach the younger children. At the end of

ChapterChapter

I'llI'll

the week, a teacher and the principal came to tell me of the amazing change in these students. They said they didn't know what I had done, but that the boys had become model students overnight.

There are many people for whom yoyo is just a fun toy. For a lot of us however, it's a critical part of who we are and how we live. I can't articulate how much of an honor it has been to have people open up and share their stories with me. Witnessing the number of ways yoyo has helped different people is beautiful. That something as simple as a spinning toy on a string could have this power is truly a wonder! Every year when yoyo club starts at school, I don't do it for the mob of kids who are there for something novel. I do it for the handful of kids for whom yoyo will become a part of their journey and help shape who they are, hopefully for the better!

Conclusion

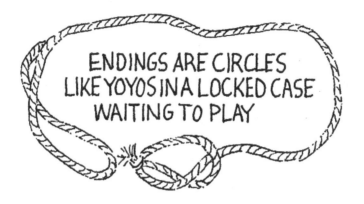

ENDINGS ARE CIRCLES
LIKE YOYOS IN A LOCKED CASE
WAITING TO PLAY

It's amazing to me how many lives have touched mine through my yoyo experiences. I treasure the people who are excited to see me at contests or who share videos of themselves performing tricks I've taught. I have made friendships that I wouldn't trade for anything.

Almost 10 years ago, I started out as a classroom teacher helping students manage a new fad. This morphed into a life-changing passion. I have journeyed through the process of learning new tricks, developing my own, and teaching them to others. My future holds many more years developing and sharing tricks. The business I continue to build will always remain focused around community-building and having fun.

The yoyo community is a beautiful cross section of society. Some of the best people I've known spend their spare time revelling in this hobby. Every day, I'm grateful to have found this passion.

I've been a competitor. I've had my foot in the door and seen a glimpse of the intensity and dedication required to make it to the top. My time on stage has been exciting and inspirational. Daily practice and learning are the best way to find inspiration. I sometimes miss it when I hit patches where my creativity has dried up and I struggle to innovate. Yet competition requires far more time and attention than I'm willing to give it. I hit my goal of winning Canadian Nationals, and that was enough for me.

My first stumbles into the business of yoyo with King Yo Star brought forth an ability and interest for sales and marketing. I caught the entrepreneur bug. I've experimented with a variety of yoyo-related projects and I suspect there will be more before I'm through. Business is exciting and challenging because it revolves around people, and people are ever fascinating.

Hands down, the best part of the yoyo world is the community. The people who gravitate towards yoyo seem to be the type of people who want to enjoy life in the company of good people. It's strange because they are from all walks of life, from biker to skater to teacher to doctor. We all just love to play with, talk about, and enjoy yoyos. It's rare to see anyone cause real problems in this community. It's rare to see the kind of drama you get in so many other places, especially when you are talking about social media. There is a layer of kindness and helpfulness that is so essential to a happy community. It's an honour to have found a home amongst this group.

Had you told me 20 years ago that I'd be writing a book about yoyos, my response would have been confusion and curiosity. The fact that I have travelled the world making friends, competing, and promoting this hobby still baffles me to this day. The yoyo is a simple toy with a long history of bringing peace in times of stress. I continue to find joy in helping friends who want to make yoyos, and giving them a leg up through advice or collaboration projects. The business has given me the excuse to travel to places I would never otherwise have visited. Iceland was magnificent, and Prague so full of history. Yoyo has so many more places to take me and people to bring into my life.

Well, that was a whirlwind tour of the yoyo world. The reality is that most of us wear multiple hats and identify with a combination of labels. I'm sure there are many more ways to categorize yoyoers that I missed when compiling this book. This is a starting point, not a definitive guide. I offer this book to prospective yoyoers, to help you figure out where to dip your toes. For seasoned throwers, I hope I've tickled your curiosity and you find yourself with a renewed desire to explore the hobby.

The people who shared their stories are why yoyo is amazing. The last decade of my life has been full of wonder at the level of peace and community I've found. There is a place for everyone, and everyone is welcome. I like to joke that yoyo is for kids from ages four to one-hundred-and-four. We all love to play; it is a fundamental part of human nature. It's how we best learn and grow (ask anyone who has raised a child). I love that I get to live in an era where it's okay for grownups to be nerds, play with toys, run around in the park, and just have fun.

Now I'm off to go play!

I have some tricks to learn.

Thank you all, friends old and new.

Appendix A – Parts of a Yoyo

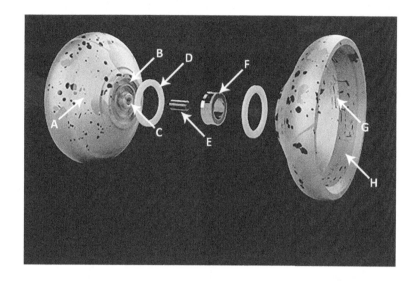

A - Gap
B - Response Groove
C - Bearing Seat
D - Response Pad
E - Axle
F - Bearing
G - Cup
H - Inner Grind Rim

Modern yoyos are a little more complicated than the old-fashioned wooden ones. Appendix A is a graphic that breaks down the parts.

Each yoyo half is machined separately on a computer controlled lathe with incredible precision. Part D - the response pad - is what helps the string grab and return the yoyo to the hand. These are usually either pre-cut silicone pads, or liquid silicone poured in and left to set.

The ball bearing has evolved with the rest of the yoyo. If you look closely you can see that there's a step down from the edges of the bearing. There are numerous variations on this design, but the idea is to help keep the string in the middle of the bearing where it won't rub against the pads on the side and slow down the spin.

You'll also run into "transaxle" or "brain" yoyos.

Transaxle yoyos have a metal axle with a plastic sleeve around it. Before ball bearings took over, this was a huge innovation in extending sleep times.

The 1990's saw the creation of the "Brain" or "Auto Return" yoyo. This design involves springs and weights built into the yoyo. When the yo-yo is thrown, a weight inside pops out to the edge and unlocks the transaxle, letting it spin freely. As the yoyo slows down the spring pops the weight back into the middle and locks the transaxle which causes the yoyo to return to the hand. It's a fun novelty for beginners, but it makes for really unpredictable play and isn't very common nowadays outside of dollar store yoyos.

Appendix B – Styles of Yoyo

Traditionally there were two styles of yoyo. 1A (for one arm) and 2A (for two arms). As players found new ways to yoyo, the naming system continued.

Here are the five main competition styles. If you aren't familiar with them, I suggest a YouTube search for "World Champion (number)A" for each style.

1A – *Single yoyo (usually unresponsive) attached with a single string to one hand. This is the most common style of yoyo and has an immense range of trick options*

2A – *2 responsive yoyos, one attached to each hand. Tricks generally involve the yoyos looping out and in again in a variety of fashions.*

3A – *2 unresponsive yoyos, one tied to each hand manipulated in a more complex fashion than 2A. Yoyos are wound and tangled together in patterns, then untangled and returned to the hand.*

4A (aka Offstring)– *The yoyo is not attached to the string. Tricks involved launching and catching the yoyo in a variety of ways.*

5A (aka Freehand) -*A single yoyo with a dice or similar small object (aka a counterweight) tied to the end instead of a finger. The yoyo and the counterweight are manipulated together to create tricks.*

These 5 are the standard contest divisions. There is a much longer list of trick styles that is ever evolving as players innovate. Double dragon is like 1A, but two strings are tied to a single yoyo. Full Loop is a mix of 4A and 5A, where the ends of the string are tied to make a giant loop with the yoyo unattached and manipulated with the loop. A quick search on the internet for "styles of yoyo play" will help you find the full list and a search on google will give you plenty of examples of these styles in action!

Appendix C – 77 Rules for Yoyo Players

Years ago yoyoer Ed Haponik wrote these rules out in his blog. I think they are awesome, so I got his permission to reprint them here for you. If you don't know who Ed is, find his Instagram and be amazed.

77 Rules for Yoyo Players -By Ed Haponik

1. Learn to loop. With two hands.

2. When you play yo-yo in public, look up. Be aware of your surroundings. Say "hi" to the people who look at you in wonder. Say "hi" to those who look at you with disdain.

3. Be generous with your time, and with your toys. If you have the means, at every event you attend, give something away to someone (who does not ask).

4. Understand the differences between yo-yoing for yourself in your room, yo-yoing for judges at a contest, and yo-yoing for a small child at the park.

5. Try to find and play yo-yo's that come from every decade of the past century. Appreciate their differences (and similarities).

6. When performing for an audience, always look better than they do.

7. Be proud you're a yo-yo player. Have pity for those who think you shouldn't be.

8. Never act like yo-yoing is a big inconvenience. No one's making you do it.

9. Be prepared to walk the dog on command. Always.

10. Never blame the judges. Maintain the attitude that, if you had REALLY won, it wouldn't have been up to them at all.

11. Hit a true laceration on a stock Renegade. Fly-away dismount.

12. Don't talk about how 'so-and-so' is a lousy player (or human being) if you're unwilling to bring it to them personally.

13. Don't confront someone about being a lousy player (or human being) unless you're right. And be sure you understand the consequences.

14. When you're getting paid to yo-yo, be on time and do your job with a smile.

15. Don't yo-yo with the goal of being admired. don't worry over whether you're 'somebody in the yo-yo community'. Be 'somebody in real life' and then be the same person in the yo-yo community.

16. Recognize that you don't really know very many tricks at all. This should make you feel inspired rather than pathetic.

17. Find a mentor. Or twelve. No need to be explicit about it, but they should know who they are and what they mean to you.

18. Stay up all night playing yo-yo.

19. Compete. Ladder, freestyles, best trick, or whatever. Register, pay, and support the contest.

20. Carry a paperclip in your wallet.

21. Don't accept sponsorship from a company you don't absolutely love.

22. Carve a palm tree on a yo-yo using a pocket knife.

23. Understand how your yo-yo's work. Be able to maintain them.

24. Never begrudge your dings. Not in yo-yo. Not in life.

25. Respect the venue.

26. Meet the masters (national or otherwise). Shake their hands and thank them for making yo-yoing something more. Make that YOUR goal.

27. Take care of your hands, wrists, body, and mind. When those things fail, so will your yo-yoing.

28. Don't go out of your way to vilify this or that company. Support the ones that you feel benefit the community and yo-yoing in general. That's enough.

29. Travel to a contest alone.

30. Travel to a contest in an overfull car.

31. Respect your elders.

32. Don't fiddle obsessively with your bearings. They'll do their job if you let them.

33. It's one thing to be awed, but don't be intimidated by yo-yo players, regardless of their skill.

34. Learn to snap-start.

35. Find a yo-yo that you can't play well at all. Play it exclusively for a month.

36. Go to worlds.

37. Be able to do enough of each style to wow the uninitiated.

38. Do something else. Take up an instrument. Knit. Do card tricks. Shoot skeet. Something.

39. Make yourself useful at contests. Help set up. Help clean up.

40. Don't be careless with other peoples' yo-yo's. Don't be overprotective of yours.

41. Own an old wood yo-yo.

42. If you bring a bunch of yo-yo's somewhere, it will be understood that you want people to see them and be impressed. Don't be surprised when they aren't.

43. Pass out on a yo-yoer's floor in delighted exhaustion.

44. Learn all you can about every major player from every era of yo-yoing's history. This art is FULL of fascinating characters.

45. Be neither proud nor ashamed of your collection.

46. Don't seek to be someone else's favorite player. Seek to be your own favorite player. And in that regard, NEVER succeed.

47. Don't leave home without it.

48. Learn to twist your own string.

49. Play responsive, but don't act like it's a big deal.

50. Practice more. Post less.

51. Develop yourself such that someday, if you should find yourself in a room surrounded by your heroes, you will be pleasantly surprised to find that you belong.

52. Invent a trick. Hell, invent so many tricks that finding a way to record them becomes a necessity.

53. Don't hide behind the mantle of an 'online persona'. That has zero to do with being a yo-yoer.

54. Run a contest or event. Make it a benefit to the companies that are willing to sponsor it. Make it a benefit to the players who come and spend their day.

55. Don't treat yo-yo's as if they're people, or vice versa.

56. Make a video. Before you publish or hype it, make certain that it's something that you would want to watch all the way through, even if the yo-yoer were some random guy you've never met.

57. Yo-yo transcends gender, and yet the vast majority of yo-yoers are male. Respect and appreciate the few girls and women brave enough to wade through all the smelly aggro testosterone to do their thing.

58. Find a globe. Locate 'the other side of the world'. Befriend a yo-yo player from there (or as close as you can manage).

59. At one point, you were just starting out. Whether it was last week or 50 years ago, remember that time. Treat those who are learning the basics with care. Answer their questions, help them with string tension, and don't act like they need to get in line to kiss your boot.

60. Acquire a yo-yo from shinobu, eric wolff, or john higby.

61. Always have a spare string on you.

62. Have more than one gear. Go fast when it's time to go fast. Go slow when it's time to go slow. Understand when it's appropriate to play simply and when it's best to be strange and complicated.

63. Don't set too much store by contest results. At their MOST valid, they give an idea of who played the best for three minutes, on one given day. Respect everyone who can get up there with poise and intent.

64. Don't define yourself by your style. Instead, let your style be defined by your spirit.

65. Treat every throw as if it's your last. (throw today.)

66. Treat every throw as if it's your first. (throw forever.) The two are not actually contradictory.

67. Mine yoyoing's history for forgotten tricks. Find the invisible threads connecting them to modern play.

68. Find a player whose tricks you find "ugly". learn one of those tricks and try to see it in the way they do.

69. Be able to make any yo-yo look radical.

70. Pay attention to how others play. Take in their tricks as you would listen to their stories.

71. When binding into a snag, don't curse into your breath. laugh and throw a few shoot-the-moons before fixing it.

72. When asked whether you're throwing a "trick yo-yo" or one with a motor in it, respond with patience rather than scorn.

73. It's said that "those who know don't post." Seek out those who know.

74. Who's better - Barney Akers or Hiroyuki Suzuki? Recognize the insanity inherent in trying to compare two masters (or anyone really).

75. Don't feel compelled to plaster a huge smile on your face every time you yo-yo, but do try to take some joy from throwing.

76. Throw everywhere: on mountains, at the beach, on the airplane, or in line at the DMV. Yo-yoing is a momentary fist-bump with reality and suits most occasions.

77. Disregard these rules. Make up your own rules and make allowances for those who won't play or live by them.

Share Your Story!

Do you have a story to share?

I would love to write a follow-up book full of stories from other members of the world-wide yoyo community, or those who are just now finding it and joining in the fun!

Anything you have to share is welcome!

I'm particularly interested in stories from the 1990's yoyo boom as I'm considering a book about that era.

If you are interested, please email
mryoyothrower@gmail.com
with your story!

Acknowledgements

No artist operates in a vacuum. This book is the result of many, many discussions with other professionals, business owners and yoyoers in general. It would not exist without the support of the yoyo community as a whole, members of which inspire me to keep helping the sport grow.

- My wife, Andra, continues to not only tolerate my strange hobby, but revel in it. She has read this book more times than anyone should and has been extraordinarily patient as I disappear into my laptop to write "just a few more sentences."

- My mom for my love of reading and passion for teaching.

- My dog Dandy has also shown great patience, sitting and watching me work at the computer instead of taking him out for his 5th walk of the day.

- Susan Currie for being the friend that talked me through the tough times and helped me tear the book apart and put it back together when I was stuck and ready to give up. She gave me the kick in the pants needed to keep going.

- Christopher Francz for the amazing chapter art

- Author Jeyn Roberts for telling me writing about yoyos was a good idea, and slogging through my first draft and turning it into something resembling coherent thoughts.

- Chris Kukucha, that teacher we all have who truly inspires and pushes us. I took five political science classes with him. He made it his priority to make sure his students not only knew the subject material, but taught his class to <u>write</u> and write well.

- All of the yoyoers who helped read through and share feedback of many drafts, I couldn't have done this without you. Chris Francz who crafted the delightful comics at the beginning of each chapter. Cameron Blair for coming to the rescue with designs and schematics. My team - Waylon Crase, Jordan Walker, Justin Scott Larson, Luna Harran, Tyler Hackett, and Bailey Main for all their help promoting Rain City Skills and encouraging me through this. The members of the Mr. Yoyothrower's Minions Facebook group for the endless stream of "What about this?" posts.

- Steve Brown for being the draft reader every author needs, who will say "I'm sorry, it's a mess, you did too much." Followed by "But it's full of great stuff, you've actually written 3 books here!" Well, here's #2!

- Did I mention my wife? Doesn't matter, she deserves double recognition.

About the Author

J.D. McKay, aka Mr. Yoyothrower, *is a champion yoyoer, an elementary school teacher, a musician and an author. He lives in Vancouver, Canada and has a small fluffy dog named Dandy (short for Yankee Poodle Dandy). He enjoys learning and sharing his knowledge. He also really likes cookies and eats far too many whilst sitting in coffee shops writing stories.*

You can join his mailing list and more at **jdmckay.com** *or find him on Facebook and Instagram.*

Looking for a yoyo? Head to **www.raincityskills.com** *to chek out Mr. Yoyothrower's brand of quirky, fun yoyos. Then head to* **www.mryoyothrower.com** *for over 400 videos teaching the art of yoyo.*

Don't forget to check out **How to Run a Boutique Yoyo Business** *to learn a little more about the modern world of yoyo!*

Autographs and Stickers

Here are a couple extra pages you can use to collect autographs from your favourite yoyo people or the stickers you collect as you travel through the yoyo world!

Autographs and Stickers

Autographs and Stickers

Autographs and Stickers

Autographs and Stickers